U.S. Foreign Policy in the Middle East

U.S. Foreign Policy in the Middle East

The Role of Lobbies and Special Interest Groups

Janice J. Terry

Pluto Press

LONDON • ANN ARBOR, MI

First published 2005 by Pluto Press
345 Archway Road, London N6 5AA
and 839 Greene Street, Ann Arbor, MI 48106

www.plutobooks.com

British Library Cataloguing in Publication Data
A catalogue record for this book is available from the British Library

ISBN   0 7453 2259 X hardback
ISBN   0 7453 2258 1 paperback

Library of Congress Cataloging in Publication Data applied for

10   9   8   7   6   5   4   3   2   1

Designed and produced for Pluto Press by
Chase Publishing Services Ltd, Fortescue, Sidmouth, EX10 9QG, England
Typeset from disk by Stanford DTP Services, Northampton, England
Printed and bound in Canada by Transcontinental Printing

Contents

Acknowledgements

Many people and institutions contributed to making this book a reality. The Gerald Ford and Jimmy Carter Presidential Libraries and their outstanding staffs were unfailingly helpful and forthcoming with suggestions for further avenues of research and documentation. At the Ford and Carter Presidential Libraries particular thanks go to Drs. Don W. Wilson, David A. Horrocks and Dr. Don Schewe, Director, and archivist, Dr. James A. Yancey, Jr., respectively. Eastern Michigan University granted Faculty Research Leaves and a Sabbatical from teaching to provide the blocks of time necessary for research and writing. Dr. Gersham Nelson, Head of the EMU History and Philosophy Department, also encouraged the project. I am also grateful for a Grant-in-Aid award from the Rockefeller Archive Center to conduct research in their extensive holdings.

The late Egyptian diplomat, Tahseen Basheer, provided an overview into Arab responses to U.S. policies as well as introducing me to a very wide range of professionals involved in influencing foreign policy. A generation of scholars and journalists owe him a profound debt of gratitude for his assistance and direction. Ambassador Clovis Maksoud was similarly generous in sharing his vast knowledge and experience in the fields of diplomacy and foreign policy. Many other individuals involved with lobbies and pressure groups shared their inside knowledge and perceptions, but preferred to speak off the record.

Sally Marks is one of the main "angels" who persistently, but ever so gently, prodded me to complete the research and to synthesize the material into what hopefully is a cogent whole. However, all errors are mine alone. A round of applause is owing to Roger van Zwanenberg and Rebecca Wise of Pluto Press for their suggestions and editorial advice and to Martha Wade of Wade Management for her knowledge of all things musical. Finally, a standing ovation goes to Donald Burke, who is simply the best.

Abbreviations and Acronyms

AAI	Arab American Institute
AARP	American Association of Retired Persons
AAUG	Association of Arab American University Graduates
ADC	American-Arab Anti-Discrimination Committee
ADCRI	Anti-Discrimination Committee Research Institute
ADL	Anti-Defamation League
AEI	American Enterprise Institute
AFSC	American Friends Service Committee
AHEPA	American Hellenic Educational Progressive Association
AHI	American Hellenic Institute
AIPAC	American Israel Public Affairs Committee
ATFP	American Task Force on Palestine
AWACS	Airborne Warning and Control System
AZEC	American Zionist Emergency Council
CAIR	Council on American Islamic Relations
D-North Dakota	Democrat – North Dakota, etc.
GFL	Gerald Ford Library
IRMEP	Institute for Research: Middle Eastern Policy
JCL	Jimmy Carter Library
JDL	Jewish Defense League
LBJ	Lyndon Baines Johnson
Memri	Middle East Media Research Institute
MERIP	Middle East Research and Information Project
MESA	Middle East Studies Association
MPAC	Muslim Public Affairs Council
NAAA	National Association of Arab-Americans
NSC	National Security Council
OPEC	Organisation of Petroleum Exporting Countries
PACs	Political Action Committees
PHRC	Palestine Human Rights Campaign
PLO	Palestine Liberation Organization
R-Cal	Republican – California, etc.
R&D	Research and Development

Rep. D.	Representative Democrat
TRNC	Turkish Republic of North Cyprus
UHAC	United Hellenic American Congress
UJA	United Jewish Appeal
WINEP	Washington Institute for Near East Policy
ZOA	Zionist Organization of America

Introduction

How does Washington decide upon and implement its foreign policy in the Middle East? What domestic and international factors are taken into consideration before decisions are made and put into practice? These questions have been hotly debated among experts and have befuddled much of the U.S. public for decades. In the aftermath of the obvious failures of U.S. foreign policy following the 9/11 attacks, the need to answer these questions has taken on even greater immediacy.

As an historian, my original approach in the search to understand and explain the process was to study the policies toward the Middle East adopted by the Ford administration, using the Ford Presidential Library as the main source of documentation. However, this soon proved impractical because most of the key documents – and indeed, the majority of everything having to do with Henry Kissinger, who was the main architect of policy during the 1970s – remain classified. But there is a wealth of material on the attempts by lobbyists and outside interest/pressure groups to influence and structure U.S. foreign policy in the Middle East. Entering through the backstage door opened up corridors for the fruitful investigation of how lobbyists operate and how the government, in particular the White House, responds to and/or ignores a myriad of lobbyists and pressure groups.

Although it is regrettable, the sensitivity of the times seems to demand a full disclosure of my own background with regard to this topic. I come to the subject as an outsider with no ethnic, religious, national, or familial ties to any of the states or peoples in the Middle East. However, my entire academic career has been devoted to the study of the region, with a particular emphasis on political development and the role of the media during the nineteenth and twentieth centuries.

This study does not detail the internal working dynamics or history of any specific lobby, interest group/organization, or individual. Nor is it an analysis of only one specific policy decision, or of a single Presidential administration. Since there are essentially no domestic U.S. lobby groups dealing with Iran, that vital nation is not included; this is not to imply that Iran does not play a key role in U.S. policy considerations, but is rather to emphasize that most decisions regarding Iran are made in coordination – albeit sometimes at cross purposes – by the State Department, Pentagon, CIA and White House. This study does provide a historic overview with specific "case studies" to explain how policies are made and what role, if any, lobbyists and pressure groups have in influencing and guiding U.S. policies in the Middle East.

I have used opera as an accessible analogy to illuminate the exceedingly complex interrelationship between the players who create foreign policy. The case studies used to underpin the analysis are taken predominantly from the Ford and Carter administrations. I have also been fortunate enough to interview numerous professionals, paid lobbyists, pressure group leaders and career foreign service officers and experts from the Middle East (Egypt, Jordan, Lebanon, Syria, Cyprus, Israel and Palestine), as well as Washington insiders. These experts have been unfailingly helpful in sharing their personal experiences and observations. The Ford and Carter presidencies are particularly appropriate choices for the study of lobbies and foreign policy. Each was a one-term president, one a Republican and the other a Democrat. Both dealt with the same or similar foreign policy issues. In spite of their very different personal styles and backgrounds, Ford and Carter ended up adopting analogous policies in the Middle East.

Ford's major involvement regarding the Middle East entailed the two Sinai disengagement accords, the courting of Anwar Sadat out of the Soviet orbit, the anti-Arab Boycott campaign and the ongoing occupation and division of Cyprus following the 1974 Turkish invasion. Cyprus provides an instructive contrast to the influence of lobbies/pressure groups on policy outside the parameters of the highly emotive Arab Israeli conflict. Under Carter the main issues were the Camp David Accords and subsequent Egyptian Israeli peace treaty, the ongoing Arab Israeli conflict, Cyprus, Iran and, to a much lesser extent, the anti-Arab Boycott campaign.

The analysis critiques lobbyists – their failures and successes – as well as specific policy decisions. The failures and the comparatively fewer successes of pro-Arab groups are examined in a critical light. Israeli and Zionist lobby campaigns and policies are held up to similar scrutiny. In their desire to prevent debate on the highly emotional history and impact of the Arab Israeli conflict, some supporters of Israel have sought to equate any criticism of Israel or Zionism with anti-Semitism. While this has served the narrow political interests of Israel as well as having a chilling effect, it has prevented the public – and voters – from understanding the influence lobbyists and pressure groups have had on U.S. foreign policy. In fact, it should be self-evident that criticism of specific Israeli actions and policies is no more anti-Semitic than it is to claim that opposition to Iraq's invasion of Kuwait in 1990 was anti-Arab or anti-Islamic, or opposition to the U.S. invasion and occupation of Iraq in 2003 is necessarily anti American.[1]

To provide a context for examining the role of lobbies in U.S. policy formation, Chapter 1 introduces the process whereby foreign policy decisions are made. The next two chapters provide a backdrop or stage set, focusing on the media and the prevalent cultural images of the Middle East in U.S. society as well as providing some explanations for the shortcomings of media coverage, particularly on international issues. Chapter 3 describes the negative stereotyping of Arabs and Muslims. Briefly, there is a systemic predisposition by the American public toward favorable policies to given nations, for example Greece and Israel, and a concomitant negative predisposition toward Arabs and Muslim nations. Thus the later must counter negative stereotypes and attitudes before they can even begin to present positive images. This situation was intensified by the 9/11 attacks.

Chapter 4 describes the techniques and strategies used by all lobby and special interest groups. The key factor of finance is also discussed. Chapter 5 is an "overture" that uses Cyprus as the main theme or case study of a successful lobby effort by Greek Americans to force changes in U.S. policies regarding Cyprus and Turkey. Chapters 6 and 7 introduce the various pro-Arab and pro-Israeli lobbies and special interest groups. The discussion then continues, in more or less chronological order, with the Ford administration, the major anti-Arab Boycott campaign and ends with the Carter presidency. The conclusion summarizes the positive and negative impacts of lobby groups on foreign policy from the 1970s to the present. The pressure special interest groups bring to bear on politicians and officials responsible for the formation and implementation of policies in the Middle East affects all Americans, as well as the international community. Thus it is crucial, especially in a democratic state, for citizens to understand the strengthens and weaknesses of lobbies and to demand that their representatives adopt policies in the best interests of the entire society.

I

The Libretto: Making Foreign Policy

Operas are the harmonious blend of numerous, seemingly disparate, elements (score, libretto, singers, stage sets, orchestra, conductor, stage directors, publicity, ticket sales, rehearsals). So, too, foreign policy evolves out of a complex interplay among a number of government agencies including the President, Department of State, Pentagon, CIA, Congress, and the National Security Council (NSC). Since World War II, Congressional involvement has generally declined while that of the President, his close advisers and, in particular, the NSC has grown.[1] Created during the Truman administration, the NSC began as a small group of senior experts who served in a purely advisory capacity to the president. Since NSC advisers are appointed to office, they report directly to the president and are not constrained by the political considerations that influence politicians – especially presidents who enter the White House already running for a second term. By the 1970s, the power of the NSC was so great that Zbigniew Brzezinski viewed it as responsible for the "architecture," with the State Department performing the "acrobatics" of foreign policy.[2] From the Vietnam war to the 2003 war on Iraq, presidents and their advisers have tried to avoid public scrutiny or involvement in foreign affairs, often operating secretly through closed-door negotiations. Some have even relegated Secretaries of State to stand-in roles, giving the leads to White House officials such as Henry Kissinger under Ford,[3] Brzezinski under Carter and Dick Cheney/Donald Rumsfeld under George W. Bush.

Although Congress exerts enormous power in the key areas of foreign aid and arms appropriations, presidents and their advisers have come to consider foreign policy as their exclusive purview. They also largely determine who has access to the decision making process. In short, a small elite group, acting from the top down, generally makes foreign policy.[4] This elite group prefers having the stage to themselves, with as small a cast of supporting singers as possible.

As the imperial presidency evolved, notably under Johnson and Nixon, the president came to play a crucial role in the development and conduct of foreign policy. Under some administrations, as with Henry Kissinger during Gerald Ford's presidency, the Secretary of

State acts as the main architect of foreign policy. At other times, that role is played by the National Security Adviser as with Brzezinski in the Carter administration, or the Vice President and Secretary of Defense under George W. Bush. Although this "multiple advocacy"[5] provides diversity of opinion, it also makes determining who actually formulates foreign policy extremely difficult.

In a president's perfect world, decisions would be based on the nation's best interests within the context of economics and geo-politics. Obviously, it is not a "perfect" world. When making foreign policy, presidents, as products of the political system, must consider domestic demands. In practice, politics and domestic pressures may take precedence over cold, hard "realpolitik."

In the 1970s when President Ford was in the midst of negotiations to bring Egypt and Anwar Sadat into the American orbit, he directly addressed this issue during a meeting with the National Security Council. His remarks spotlight two main aspects of U.S. foreign policy in the Middle East and the importance of domestic lobbies.

> I will tell you briefly about my record in Congress where Israel is concerned. It was so close that I have a black reputation with the Arabs. I have always liked and respected the Israeli people. They are intelligent and dedicated to the causes in which they believe. They are dedicated to their religion, their country, their family and their high moral standards. I admire and respect them. And I have never been so disappointed as to see people I respect unable to see that we are trying to do something for their interest as well as for our own. But in the final analysis our commitment is to the United States.
> Vice President Nelson Rockefeller: "Hear, hear."[6]

In this scenario, Ford clearly enunciates the foundation of foreign policy – self-interest. But his rhetoric also reveals a curious, but not unusual "Orientalist" tendency to generalize, in the most sweeping and positive terms, about the Israelis, while tacitly, if not explicitly, denigrating Arabs and Muslims. This almost visceral pro-Israeli and anti-Arab position will be explored in greater depth in the following chapters.

Newly elected presidents are most likely to consider policy shifts during their first few months in office. New presidents often announce that they are "reassessing" Middle East policy. During this short time frame, lobbyists have a small "window of opportunity" to push their proposed agendas and to offer suggestions for policy changes.

Obviously, the groups with well-established linkages, sympathizers in key administrative posts and liaisons directly with the White House have the advantage.

The element of time is an important component of any lobbying effort. A campaign timed in the months just prior to a presidential election may bolster, or in some cases harm, a lobbying effort. Lobbyists and pressure groups must weigh the time factor carefully, gauging the chances for the success or failure of their agendas. No politician wants to be identified with a failed program. An unsuccessful campaign damages the very cause it seeks to promote. The Clinton health care initiative demonstrated that a failed campaign sets back a cause by months or even years.

OPINION POLLS

To encourage ticket sales and large audiences, opera companies publicize new productions and their star artists through mass mailings, stylish brochures and advertising campaigns. To ensure domestic support for their foreign policy, presidents must also communicate and explain the issues to the American public. This may even involve massive public relations campaigns waged through the media in "fireside chats" and radio and television appearances. To gauge public attitudes on specific policy issues, presidential advisers also pay close attention to public opinion polls. They routinely monitor poll results, noting the variations of opinion among different ethnic groups, particularly Jewish Americans.[7] Based on a 1975 poll of Americans on a wide range of Middle East issues, one assessment emphasized that:

> The public and the leaders are leary of an outside imposed solution to the Middle East conflict and would prefer that the conflict be settled by and among the antagonists ... In short, most Americans think it will take close to a miracle ... for peace in the Middle East.[8]

Advisers not only follow and summarize polls, they also make policy recommendations based on their assessments of public opinion. Thus on the basis of the aforementioned poll, one insider bluntly recommended that Ford and the Republican party adopt an openly pro-Israeli stance in the forthcoming 1976 election campaign and concluded that:

From the perspective of the coming elections, it is apparent that a policy which hurts or appears to hurt Israel and appeases Arab demands will carry a stiff political price in the United States, and a price which the Republican party should not be asked to pay. But it would also be a lost opportunity to rally the American public behind a country widely perceived as a reliable, democratic ally at a time when we have so few such allies left around the world.[9]

Recognizing the role polls play in politics, especially in election years, Israel and its supporters also closely monitor poll results on the Middle East. Lobbyists and pressure groups study how polls are taken and use them as one measure of the success or failure of their individual lobby campaigns.[10] If a poll indicates public support for a given policy or nation, lobbyists use the findings as leverage to persuade politicians to vote for or against forthcoming legislation, arms deals or financial aid. They may also argue, based on poll results, that voters will support or oppose a candidate based on his or her record on specific policies involving the Middle East.

VOTING

Although most Americans believe that it takes hundreds of thousands of people to influence foreign policy, it can be demonstrated that only 5,000–10,000 committed activists can have a substantial impact. Two systemic factors make this astoundingly low number a realistic estimate. Just as a very small percentage of the general public attend operatic productions, only a very small percentage of citizens participate in the political system.

First, anti-Castro Cuban Americans[11] and Jewish Americans supporting Israel are the only two ethnic groups in the entire United States that have historically supported consistent, long term, and proactive lobbying efforts on issues of foreign policy. The hundreds of other ethnic or religious groups tend to react to events or issues on a case by case basis. They do not usually maintain or support ongoing lobby efforts. Thus, as will be discussed in Chapter 5, Greek Americans organized in support of Cyprus only after Turkey had invaded and occupied 40 percent of the island in 1974. Similarly, Arab Americans, especially the Lebanese, rallied in support of Lebanon after Israel had invaded in 1982. In both instances, visible and extensive campaigns led by ethnic leaders dissipated or disappeared altogether soon after the invasions and the end of full-scale hostilities. Consequently, in productions involving the Middle East, the Zionist lobby generally has the stage entirely to itself, as does the Cuban lobby with regard to Cuba. Most other Americans pay little or no attention to matters of foreign policy – unless, of course, American lives are at stake.

Secondly, most American citizens do not vote. Thus a very small proportion of highly motivated and mobilized citizens can, and do, have a disproportionate impact. Only about 70 percent of the U.S. population are eligible to vote so out of every 100 Americans 70 people are eligible to vote. Out of those 70 people only 60 percent, or 42 people, actually register. In a best case scenario only 50 percent, or 21 people, actually vote. A candidate needs only 50 percent, plus one, or eleven votes to win. Thus as Table 1.1 demonstrates, out of every 100 people a politician knows that he/she need appeal only to eleven people.

Table 1.1

Each ♀ represents 10 people		
♀♀♀♀♀♀♀♀♀♀	100 Americans	
♀♀♀♀♀♀♀	70% eligible	= 70 people
♀♀♀♀♀♀	60% registered	= 42 people
♀♀♀	50% vote	= 21 people
♀♀	50% plus one, 11 people	= victory

Participatory democracy is even less evident in presidential elections when the electoral college actually casts the votes to determine the president. As the 2000 campaign and victory of George W. Bush demonstrated, this may result in the defeat of the candidate who actually has the most votes. Since votes in the electoral college are heavily weighted in favor of five to seven largely urban states, the popular democratic system is further diminished. As the 2000 presidential election in Florida showed, bureaucratic machinations in maintaining voter registration records, dropping voters from the lists, or mishandling lists further jeopardize voting rights.[12] There is an enormous need for clearer standards and more transparency in voting methods that are overseen by non-partisan agencies, not beholden to a given political party.[13]

The methods used to select presidential candidates in primary elections are also vulnerable to special interest machinations. In selecting the presidential candidates, states may choose from three methods: the caucus system, an election paid for by the specific political party and held at the time and place of its own choosing; the closed primary, paid for by the government and held in regular polling locales, in which voters declare their party affiliation; or the open primary, paid for by the government, held at regular polling locales, in which voters may vote for either of the main parties. States select whatever system they wish and may change from year to year. Voting provisions and methods may even vary from county to county within the same state.[14] Parties and special interest groups constantly seek to select the approach that they deem most advantageous to themselves. Usually this means limiting voter participation, not by becoming more inclusive. The case of Michigan, a "power house state" presidential candidates need to win, is instructive. In 2004, it was estimated that using the caucus option at most 400,000 people, or an astonishingly low 5.8 percent of the registered Michigan voters, would select the Democratic presidential candidate. In the past, voting numbers have been much lower than even these optimistic estimates. In the 2000 election only about 20,000 Michiganders voted in the Democratic party caucus.[15] Special interest groups and lobbyists are among the chief beneficiaries of this bleak reality. Although the popular image, much touted by "get out the vote campaigns" and platitudes from politicians, is that leaders want more popular participation, the simple truth is that the lives of politicians and special interest groups are much easier so long as the public remains largely apathetic and politically passive. Thus attempts to make it far easier to register and to increase voting with Sunday elections and email voting online (especially popular among the young) have met with, at best, tepid responses from most politicians.

There is little motivation to increase public participation in either domestic or international issues. Why should a politician want to curry favor with 30 or more voters, if, at present, only eleven are necessary to be elected?[16] Just as producers heed the demands of the opera-going public by staging well-known, popular choices and acceding to the demands of big donors or "angels," politicians listen to the individuals or groups who give money to their campaigns or who engage in what is popularly called "political philanthropy." Some have even argued that presidents can only govern by working within the constraints of these interest group politics.[17]

ELECTIONS

In the 1970s two presidential advisers to Gerald Ford and Jimmy Carter explained these political realities in remarkably similar and prescient memos. Presidential adviser Robert Goldwin, described by Ford as his "resident intellectual,"[18] used public opinion polls to provide guidance for the 1976 election campaign. Goldwin's confidential memo directly addressed the issue of numbers/votes. Looking forward to the forthcoming Presidential election, Goldwin wrote:

> Of all the ethnic groups in this country, Jews take the most active interest in elections and vote more assiduously than almost any other population group. They also contribute heavily to campaigns and engage actively in work at both the national and state level ...
>
> Though less than 3 percent of the U.S. population, Jews comprise between 4 and 5 percent of the total vote. In contrast, blacks – 11 percent of the population – only account for 5 percent of the total vote.
>
> Moreover, Jews are concentrated in those populous states whose electoral vote is essential for victory in the Presidential election ...
>
> If this Administration chooses to pressure Israel, it will make U.S. policy towards her an election issue. There would be a reaction not only by the American Jewish community, whose electoral clout has been delineated above, but perhaps most important, there would likely be a negative reaction by the American voting public at large.
>
> ... From the perspective of the coming elections, it is apparent that a policy which hurts or appears to hurt Israel and appeases Arab demands will carry a stiff political price in the United States.[19]

Listening to this advice, Ford assiduously avoided making the Arab Israeli conflict a campaign issue. Nevertheless, he lost to the Democrat, Jimmy Carter, who received over 60 percent of the Jewish vote.

During Carter's term in office, Hamilton Jordan, a close, long-time friend and adviser, echoed Goldwin's earlier observations on the political realities of the U.S. system in his own confidential, "Eyes only" memo. Because Jordan feared that his memo, with its "highly sensitive subject matter,"[20] would be leaked by other high ranking White House officials, he typed it himself. In this highly revealing memo, Jordan referred to other key foreign policy issues – SALT II, Panama, Cuba, Vietnam, Africa – but focused on the Middle East and the "Role of American Jewish Community," Jordan concisely pinpointed the relevant issues, emphasizing that:

> There is a limited public understanding of most foreign policy issues.

[emphasis in original] This is certainly the case with SALT II and the Middle East. This is not altogether bad as it provides us an opportunity to present these issues to the public in an politically advantageous way ...

PUBLIC EDUCATION. Public understanding of most of these issues is very limited. To the extent these issues are understood and/or perceived by the general public, they are viewed in very simplistic terms. This is a mixed blessing. On one hand, it becomes necessary to explain complex issues to the American people. On the other hand, because these issues are not well understood, a tremendous opportunity exists to educate the public to a certain point of view. In the final analysis, I suspect that we could demonstrate a direct correlation between the trust the American people have for their President and the degree to which they are willing to trust that President's judgement on complex issues of foreign policy.[21]

In effect, Jordan recommended that the president act as his own lobbyist in matters of foreign policy. Jordan went on to detail the same techniques used by professional lobbyists and volunteer domestic pressure groups. Jordan's key assumption was that the White House could use the media to explain and gain support for foreign policy decisions. This reinforces the contention that in matters of foreign policy the media generally follows the lead of the White House, not vice versa. Presidents try to build a national consensus by getting massive media coverage and support for their foreign policy initiatives.[22]

In a narrative that might have been taken directly from Goldwin's earlier memo, Jordan also provided Carter with a detailed history and analysis of the voting patterns and pro-Israeli support among American Jews. Although there is no indication that he had access to Goldwin's memo, Jordan cited the same statistics on voting patterns and, not surprisingly, came to exactly the same conclusions about the political risks posed by taking foreign policy decisions that displeased key lobby/pressure groups. In Jordan's words:

The variance in turnout between Jewish voters and other important subgroups in the voting population is staggering and serves to inflate the importance of the Jewish voters. Again New York State is the best in point. [Emphasis in the original][23]

Jordan also noted the importance of Jewish financial support for political parties and politicians, placing this "political philanthropy" firmly within the "Jewish tradition of using one's material wealth for the benefit of others."[24]

Crucially, Jordan stressed that the pro-Zionist lobby had long recognized the public's ignorance and lack of participation on foreign policy matters.

> *The cumulative impact of the Jewish lobby is even greater when one considers the fact that their political objectives are pursued in a vacuum.*
>
> There does not exist in this country a political counterforce that opposes the specific goals of the Jewish lobby. [Emphasis in original]
>
> It is even questionable whether a major shift in American public opinion on the issue of Israel would be sufficient to effectively counter the political clout of AIPAC.[25]

Since the 1970s, when Jordan wrote the above, Arab American groups have become better organized and public opinion in favor of negotiated settlements of the Israeli-Palestinian conflict has increased. However, the political chasm between the relative power of the pro-Israeli groups and pro-Arab groups remains. The Zionist lobby works assiduously to maintain that difference by perpetuating popular historic myths about Israel and limiting, insofar as possible, more accurate or balanced accounts of the Middle East, Muslims and Arabs. It thereby establishes both the framework and terms of discourse for debate involving not only the Arab Israeli conflict, but for the entire Middle East region. Further, although almost three decades have passed since Jordan's memo to President Carter, none of his successors has challenged Jordan's conclusion regarding the overall power of AIPAC.

As demonstrated, presidents and their advisers prefer to exercise exclusive control over the formation of foreign policy. But presidents and other politicians, as much as the general public, have been socialized within the cultural milieu of U.S. society and its attitudes toward other nations and peoples. Positive public attitudes make some foreign policy decisions popular with voters; conversely, negative attitudes predispose both the government and the public toward more hostile or confrontational policies. In this context, the media obviously play a pivotal role. The prevailing negative cultural images of the Muslim and Arab worlds – popularized in much of the media – often have negative impacts on U.S. foreign policy in the Middle East. Given the structural fragmentation of foreign policy formulation, the attitudes and images held by a wide variety of public officials and politicians plays an important role in influencing what policies they support or oppose. The media and popular culture are obviously key components in forming public opinion, including that of policy makers. The following two chapters provide a brief characterization of media coverage and popular images of the Middle East and its peoples and their impact on decision makers.

2
The Score: Media and Popular Culture

Operatic lyrics are based on the rhythmic foundation of the score with melodic passages interwoven and repeated throughout the production. After the curtain comes down, listeners may leave the concert hall humming or even singing memorable selections. Similarly, media images of the Middle East, in all its multitudinous forms (news, television, movies, radio, popular magazines, academic journals and textbooks, literature and the Internet) are the equivalent to the opera's musical underpinning. Lobbyists and interest groups use and repeat, in a constant refrain, media images and representations that have already entered the public's subconscious, to influence policy. While the media in the United States assert that the coverage of Arabs, Israelis, and other Middle Eastern peoples is fair, balanced and unbiased, the facts indicate otherwise.

In his seminal work, *Orientalism*, Edward Said described the phenomenon whereby the western world created and controlled the "reality" of non-western peoples and cultures.[1] Although the negative representations of Arabs and Muslims in the news media, popular culture and academia are far too numerous and pervasive to describe here, a growing body of scholarly research exists on the topic.[2] In *Islam and the West: The Making of an Image*, Norman Daniel convincingly demonstrated that the negative depictions of Islam date back to early Christian exegesis and are therefore deeply imbedded in western culture.[3] These early representations – or more correctly misrepresentations – of Islam have echoed through the centuries down to the present. The problem is compounded by the paucity of objective modern analyses of Islam and the Arab world.

In a relatively open and free society such as the United States, news coverage can appropriately be used as a yardstick by which to measure the prevalent imagery and opinions on a given subject. Although some have argued to the contrary, it is assumed here that the media in the U.S. neither set the agenda nor make the decisions regarding foreign policy. The process whereby journalists report White House statements on foreign policy issues without critical investigation has been compared to the relationship between the passengers on a cruise ship looking at items of interest only after they have been pointed out by the captain.[4] These items are then deemed "newsworthy." Having once defined what is "news," the media proceed to maintain a so-called objectivity based on pre-defined parameters.

Noam Chomsky has described the narrowly based criteria applied in judging what is "newsworthy," as well as offering perceptive documentation of the bias, lack of objectivity and distortions of news coverage dealing with the Middle East (as well as a host of other issues).[5] Media presentations impact both public opinion and political reactions. James Fallows in *Breaking the News: How the Media Undermine American Democracy,* in addition to a host of studies by other authors, describes the impact news coverage has on the voting public.[6]

Because a handful of individuals or international corporations now own and control media communications, including cable and large television networks, motion pictures, radio stations, magazines and newspapers, a near "unanimity of view" has emerged in the presentation of all issues, not only those dealing with the Middle East.[7] In addition, some analysts have argued that corporate ownership of most media sources has made the media more conservative and prone to support the established and powerful elite.[8] Debate on the Middle East in the media is increasingly limited to a small group of commentators, often from Washington based pro-Israeli think tanks, who perform as "talking heads" and write high profile opinion and/or editorial pieces.

This narrow focus limits the repertoire or debate on all substantive issues – both domestic and international. The list of those invited to contribute op-ed pieces or to perform as experts or "talking heads" is short. Although there are over 1,000 academic specialists on the Middle East in U.S. universities they are very rarely asked to debate or discuss issues of contemporary relevance. Those that contradict the prevailing wisdom or offer "hard truths" about the region and U.S. policies quickly find themselves dropped from the guest lists.

The decline of international news coverage over the past 20 years has exacerbated the problem. In 1987 *Time* magazine devoted eleven cover stories to international issues; in 1997 it devoted only one cover story to an international event.[9] As a result, the public is increasingly unaware or entirely ignorant of crucial events in the Middle East (and other regions as well). In addition, the average citizen in the United States has little or no first hand information about any foreign nation. The decline of international coverage has also resulted in an increased

"Americanization" of the news and the "death" of solid journalism in favor of star turns and frothy, "pop" coverage.[10]

By limiting access and using their personal charisma, presidents try to manipulate news coverage to their own advantage. Some, like Richard Nixon, assiduously "vetted" journalists and news sources, while others, notably Reagan and Clinton, became experts at "working" the television media. Increased media interest in gossip and trivia has further diminished the overall quality and quantity of in-depth coverage.[11]

During the Cold War, media coverage of the Middle East was generally framed in geo-political terms, with the focus on the "inherent" nationalist and cultural differences between the West and the East. The cooperation between some Arab states and the Soviet Union, complete with unflattering and often racist images of Arabs and Arab leaders, featured prominently in news articles and feature stories. In their reviews of past coverage, some syndicated columnists have even alleged that anti-Arab bigotry was "rampant in U.S. news."[12]

In the post Cold War era this dichotomy was emphasized by Samuel Huntington in his discussions of a possible, impending civilizational conflict.[13] A host of others jumped on the Huntington bandwagon to warn about a clash of civilizations between the west and the Arab/Muslim worlds – something Huntington actually warned against.[14] In the absence of the Soviet threat, the Muslim world became the new enemy. Long before the 11 September terrorist attacks, a torrent of news analyses depicting contemporary global relationships in Manichean terms of conflict between the civilized, rational west, led by the United States, and a fanatical, barbaric Muslim world opened the floodgates for a concerted attempt to repolarize the world. Ironically, this Manichean worldview corresponded to the political ideology of some radical Islamists. Arguments about the alleged "sickness" of the Arab/Muslim world were marshaled by the neo-conservatives to justify the 2003 U.S. led war against Iraq which served U.S. self interests in the region.[15] A few examples – out of literally thousands – suffice to capture the essence of what can be characterized as a media war against Islam and the Arabs in general.

NEWS COVERAGE

Columnists regularly assert that Islam is a violent religion and that Muslims are engaged in a life and death struggle against modernity and the west. Thus news headlines and opinion pieces proclaim "The Dark Side of Islam."[16] Similar sweeping generalizations have, properly, long been unacceptable when applied to other religions, racial or ethnic groups. Because these images are so prevalent, it was not surprising that in the immediate aftermath of the 1995 Oklahoma City bombing, the media and public, primed to expect the worst from Arabs and Muslims, concluded – wrongly – that Arabs or Muslims were responsible. Only after it became abundantly clear that neither Muslims nor Arabs were responsible did some op-ed pieces, ambivalently headlined "Media jump to conclusion: Muslims did it,"[17] appear. Yet no headlines proclaimed that Timothy McVeigh was a "Christian terrorist."

Highly distorted articles purporting to detail the history of terrorism against Americans highlight attacks by Arabs or other Muslims, while ignoring killings and rapes in Latin and South America, where civilians, many of whom opposed repressive U.S. supported regimes, have been victimized on a regular basis.[18] Articles on Islamic groups such as the Palestinian Hamas are similarly slanted. For example, a lead article in the Sunday Week in Review section of the *New York Times*, the "paper of record," bluntly alleged, "The Red Menace Is Gone. But Here's Islam." The photograph accompanying this feature showed a close-up of a menacing, dark-eyed male, identified in a small caption not as a member of Hamas – but as the Ayatollah Khomeini.[19] The *New York Times* subsequently ran two long, lead stories on Hamas; the first appeared under the headline, "Terror Isn't Alone as a Threat to Mideast Peace";[20] a second, a front-page lead article, featured a photograph of Hamas members sitting under anti-Israeli graffiti depicting a fist plunging a knife into a Star of David. Although these articles described the social and welfare activities of Hamas and mentioned (but only in passing) that a mere 5 percent of its income went to armed struggle, the initial impact and emphasis was on the violent, negative aspects of the organization. Conversely, the media do not accord Arab, particularly Palestinian, victims of terrorism the same extensive coverage that is given to the death of Israeli children. Indeed, there is an "undercurrent of anti-Palestinian animosity – ... in the media and even to some extent in the government – that is surprising in its virulence. Perceptions rather than reality have governed American thinking."[21]

Realistically, fully six years before the Bush administration proclaimed war against Islamic terrorism in 2001, the media had already done so. Some may allege that the media was merely prescient, but in face of pervasive public ignorance about events in the Middle East, it was also a self-fulfilling prophecy, particularly since popular culture disseminates similarly distorted images.

POPULAR CULTURE

Distortions and hostile stereotypes of Muslims and Arabs are found throughout popular culture in the West. Since numerous studies have documented this negative stereotype only a few examples are necessary to set the stage.[22]

In the contemporary era, the novel and film *Exodus* (New York: Bantam Books, 1958) by Leon Uris molded the attitudes toward the Arab Israeli conflict of an entire generation of Americans. Although supposedly based on events that are "a matter of public record," *Exodus* popularized many myths regarding Palestine, Israel and the Arab world. *Exodus* has been characterized as "priceless" for Israeli public relations.[23] The images and myths popularized as "truths" in *Exodus* helped early lobbyists and pressure groups for Israel gain support among both elected officials and opinion makers. Uris embellished these stereotypic images and distortions 30 years later in his virulently anti-Arab, anti-Muslim best-selling novel, *The Haj* (New York: Bantam Dell Publishing, 1984). Although critics routinely condemn works that are offensive to other ethnic or religious groups, they often fail to do so when the stereotypes are used to depict Arabs or Muslims. Thus reviewers typically praise murder mysteries featuring American/African American/Israeli protagonists triumphing over evil fascists and Muslims without mentioning the stereotypic, shallow or even openly racist depictions found in such novels.[24]

These distortions are not simply confined to pulp fiction. They routinely appear in more critically acclaimed works as well. For example, Nobel Prize winning author V.S. Naipaul's *Among the Believers: An Islamic Journey* (1981) was adjudged "A brilliant report" and "The most notable work on contemporary Islam to have appeared in a very long time," in spite of its distortions and errors. Naipaul imparts an overwhelming negative tone for anything Muslim or traditional; his reportage on Africa or other global southern regions is similarly distorted. Yet the *Sunday Times* (London) not only agreed with his conclusions but went so far as to allege that Naipaul, who was "raised in colonial Trinidad … knows how a simple rural economy stunts the soul."[25] The reader is left to decide for him/herself whether London and New York could not be similarly soul killing.

ACADEMIC JOURNALS AND JOURNALS OF OPINION

Because the negative treatment of Islam and Arabs is so prevalent, it is not surprising that it is replicated in textbooks and scholarly journals as well. In academic fields, the problem is twofold. First, the low level of knowledge about the Middle East results in factual errors or distorted depictions and second, scholars whose works present conclusions contradicting or challenging the prevailing academic discourse often find it difficult or impossible to publish in mainstream journals or presses. For example, in the 1950s even the prestigious Rockefeller Foundation was unable to persuade commercial or university presses to publish an important scholarly study on the Muslim Brethren.[26] Presses rejected the study on several grounds, including: it was too biased, it might have been written by a member of the Brethren (it was not), or it had no commercial interest. Publishers failed to explain in what way the study was biased, other than it dealt with the topic of Islam, or why a study authored by a member of the Brethren was unacceptable for publication. In fact, the study was based on sound scholarly research, provided a balanced presentation and reached conclusions that hold up well some 50 years later. Although the book was ultimately printed in the Arab world, it was not widely distributed in the United States, thereby failing to reach the very audience that most needed to be informed about this major Islamic movement whose impact reverberates throughout the world to the present day.

In contrast, Joan Peters' *From Time Immemorial: The Origins of the Arab-Jewish Conflict* (1984), a book replete with historic errors and distortions, not only found a mainstream publisher, but was fulsomely praised and endorsed by critics. In the publicity blitz surrounding the book's publication, Saul Bellow, Elie Wiesel, Arthur Goldberg and a host of other high profile personalities recommended it as a sold historic recreation of the Arab Israeli conflict.[27] Highly reputable scholars, most notably Albert Hourani and Norman Finkelstein, subsequently dissected the many historical errors, slanted or misquoted statistics and distortions upon which their book was based.[28] But their scholarly refutations had little impact on the general public and were not commensurate with the initial media blitz for the book that was even recommended reading for high ranking officials in the White House.

Western academics set the agenda for what are considered important subjects for research and discussion. At this juncture, it is important to emphasize that such constrictions (dare one say censorship?) are not limited merely to studies of the Middle East. Large, mainstream publishing houses, often owned by corporate media giants, are reluctant to publish works that contradict the prevailing scholarly or popular "wisdom" or discourse. During the 1990s, the cancellation of Anastasia Karakasidou's *Fields of Wheat, Rivers of Blood*, a scholarly account of nationalism and ethnicity in Greece, by Cambridge University Press, is a case in point.

Given the narrow scope of intellectual discourse on the Middle East, it is not surprising that textbooks and major journals of opinion print errors of fact or highly misleading descriptions of the region and its peoples. Although there have been concerted efforts to expunge the worst errors and distortions, resources on the Middle East for students from the elementary through secondary levels are generally poor.

Thus authors of one major text alleged that Muhammad "developed a faith of his own" and generalized that "it is customary for Muslim women to wear black veils in public."[29] It is almost impossible to imagine a text saying that Christ developed a faith of his own. Nor, obviously, do all Muslim women wear veils. Similarly, texts routinely publish photographs of veiled women or *bedu* on camels, with no attribution of where or when the photos were taken; nor do they provide information about the differences in the dress and attitudes between urban and rural women. Errors of basic historic facts are even more common. One text gave 1920 as the date for the creation of the Jewish state (1948), omitted any discussion of the British Mandate period of Palestine (1920s–1948) and failed to mention the Palestinians by name at all. Other major errors included citing 1973 as the date Saddam Hussein became dictator of Iraq, not 1979 when President Bakr resigned. The same text declared Iraq had won the Iran–Iraq War when actually the long war of attrition had no winners and was a human and economic disaster for both countries.[30]

Articles on Islam and the Middle East in leading journals of opinion reflect similar bias. The scholarly argument that a monolithic Islamic world, perhaps first enjoined by Samuel Huntington in "The Clash of Civilizations?," was poised for a violent confrontation with the western, largely Christian world became a popular script for academic debate.[31] Although Graham E. Fuller and Ian O. Lesser in *A Sense of Siege: The Geopolitics of Islam and the West* (Boulder, Co.: Westview Press, 1995), demolished many of the inaccuracies and fallacies embedded in at least some of Huntington's thesis, innumerable scholars and journalists continued to enlarge upon it. Even the normally staid *Foreign Affairs* could not resist the sensationalized title, "The Islamic Cauldron," for its issue devoted to the Middle East and a possible confrontation with the West. In this issue, Milton Viorst provided – as usual – a balanced and well-researched description of "Sudan's Islamic Experiment." On the other hand, the issue also included the obituary, by Amos Perlmutter, on "The Oslo accord's death," or "The Israel-PLO Accord is Dead."[32] While it was true that Oslo was "dead" by 2001, it was certainly premature to declare it so in 1995. Was this yet another self-fulfilling prophecy?

Authors and publishers argue that such distortions are based on objective political realities and the reader's thirst for exoticism. However, in a democratic society, the problems posed by difficulty of access and the lack of vigorous public debate on major Middle East issues pose major questions of academic integrity. It also makes the formation of cogent, rational agendas for foreign policy, especially in the Middle East, particularly susceptible to lobbying efforts.

The government and media each perpetuate myths, distortions and stereotypes about Muslims and Middle Eastern peoples. As the White House sets the foreign policy agenda and communicates it to the media in specific images, so too do the media communicate these images or exaggerations to the general public. The public, in turn, unconsciously assimilates these images which then form the basis of negative or positive attitudes toward specific peoples, leaders or nations. On the basis of these images and attitudes, public pressure or support is directed to the White House and Congress. Finally, the White House "responds" by communicating its agenda to the media. This cycle constantly repeats itself thereby creating a form of synergism, in which the impact of each act increases so that the total effect is far greater than the sum of its parts.

The operatic drama of foreign policy is played out in tune with the media score. Foreign policy professionals and politicians are no more immune to the impact of the music than the audience or public. Next the spotlight will be turned on how these images and distortions resonate in government documents, background materials and official statements by both elected and appointed high-ranking officials.

3
The Stage Set: Images and Attitudes

Stage sets, intrinsic parts of musical productions, create the mood to prepare the audience for what they are about to see and hear. Similarly, the drama of U.S. foreign policy in the Middle East is played out before a cultural backdrop projected by the media. As noted in the previous chapter, the cultural climate reinforces society's mental representations or images. Foreign policy professionals are no more immune to its impact than is the general public. Stereotypes and prejudice, defined as preconceived judgments and opinions about groups as distinguished from individuals within the group, evolve from these preconceived images. The following discussion demonstrates how decision-makers at all levels have been predisposed to either positive or negative attitudes about specific peoples or groups in the Middle East.

It has been posited that cultural stereotypes can be automatically activated in a process that some psychologists call a "default response."[1] White House and State Department documents dealing with foreign policy and foreign leaders reveal what might well be termed a "default response."

Some observers, most notably Robert Kaplan in a lead article in *Atlantic Monthly* and his book *The Arabists: The Romance of an American Elite*, have portrayed the State Department as heavily tilted toward the Arab/Muslim world.[2] Kaplan repeats many of the old shibboleths about the "romance" between Arabic speaking diplomats who, having lived in the Middle East among the Arabs, have become entranced by the beauty and simplicity of the desert. These experiences supposedly blind them to the real interests of the United States. Kaplan labels Arabs and the so-called Arabists as "self-delusionary." Kaplan's sub-text is that only diplomats who favor Israel act rationally and in the best interest of the United States.

Setting aside, for a moment, the argument that it is in the best interest of the United States to favor Israel, the validity of Kaplan's allegations regarding the "Arabists" is worth further examination. Although some diplomats have urged the United States to foster closer relations with selected Arab governments, they have done so not because they are apologists for the Arabs, but out of firm convictions that to do so is in the best interest of the United States. Historically, U.S. foreign policy in the Middle East has had four main goals: to secure the free flow of oil (preferably at the lowest possible price); to improve relations with friendly Arab/Turkish/Iranian regimes on a bilateral basis; to prevent the Middle East from becoming a sphere of interest of any other foreign nation (particularly the Soviet Union during the Cold War); and to support the continued existence of the state of Israel. With the end of the Cold War, the U.S. has also fostered the globalization and privatization of the economies of all the states in the region. Although it has been a source of bitter dispute with some arguing that the U.S. has consistently favored Israel, others have posited that the U.S. has had an ongoing commitment to a fair and even-handed resolution of the Arab Israeli conflict.[3] The inherent contradictions between fulsome U.S. support for Israel and its attempts to placate Arab demands for self-determination for the Palestinians remain a source of ongoing tension.

The advocacy of a balanced policy, particularly regarding the Arab Israeli conflict, by some State Department professionals is not analogous to an alliance with or loyalty to the Arab world. Diplomats with extensive knowledge and experience in the Arab/Muslim world have repeatedly warned Washington of the dangers inherent in ignoring Arab sensibilities, particularly on the Palestine issue. These professionals have also reported, in factual detail, what Arab leaders have told them. However, diplomats who have told the "hard truths" have sometimes found their professional careers in peril. Noting these problems, one ambassador wrote in 1979:

> It was dangerous to report unpalatable truths when Senator McCarthy reigned; under Kissinger it became fatal to report facts inconsistent with his views or wishes. Those who survived in the State Department were those who adjusted.
>
> I am even more worried now by what appears to be an extraordinary misunderstanding about Arab attitudes toward the Palestinian state ... The Arabs are convinced that there must be a state sooner or later or there will be no peace.[4]

After almost 30 years, the ambassador's observation and warning remain true and can hardly be construed as the views of a "romantic."

Further research indicates that, far from being mesmerized by the Arab world, many "Arabists" or experts share an Orientalist vision of the Middle East. Although some State Department assessments and recommendations regarding the Middle East are pragmatic, others are couched in highly superficial or general terms and include surprisingly light-hearted or even blatantly biased language. In the 1960s, a top-level official in the Johnson White House recommended William Polk for the position of U.S. Ambassador to Egypt because "he knows all the key Gyppos and is highly regarded by them."[5]

Excerpts from Polk's policy analysis on Egypt and Israel, drawn up for the White House, is a mixture of sweeping generalities and specifics:

> Since we cannot, apparently, destroy Nasser or replace him with a viable and more moderate government and since we do not want him to rely completely upon the USSR ... we ... assist Egyptian development.
>
> ... Keeping the UAR from harming our interests is a more complex and frustrating job ...
>
> We now work at this task in various ways: Where UAR activities appear to traduce significant U.S. interests, we employ force ... where Egyptian actions can be internationalized, we bring UN pressures ...
>
> ... *Has this paid off?* [emphasis in original] ... The U.S. continues to use Wheelus [airforce base in Libya], draw oil on highly profitable (about 80% return on investment yearly) terms, use the airspace and transit facilities of the Arab countries, send its ships through Suez and avoid a large-scale Arab-Israeli clash ...
>
> The Arabs believe that the weak cannot afford to be generous or considerate.[6]

Polk goes on to warn of the dangers inherent in a possible arms race and Israel's impending nuclear capabilities. "But we must continue to seek ways, including stern action, to halt the Middle Eastern arms race before it reaches the nuclear stage."[7] These are scarcely the recommendations of a professional blinded to the realities of the Middle East. The tenor of the language in both the aforementioned job recommendation and policy statement is hardly one of admiration, let alone esteem, for the Arab world. Nor is the analysis in any way based on unrealistic assessments or recommendations. Subsequent reports by a wide range of officials follow the same pattern.

Although summaries and biographic data provided by the Office of Central Reference/CIA are often fulsome and highly nuanced, they are distributed on a selective basis. They are not commonly received by political appointees in the White House, who often know little or nothing about foreign leaders or the history of individual foreign nations. As a rule, political appointees receive "canned" one to two page biographies that are provided on a regular basis, particularly prior to state visits or meetings with foreign dignitaries. Because they often vary little from year to year, or even from administration to administration, errors, distortions, or omissions are repeated over and over again.

Even a cursory comparison of the biographies or reports on European leaders, Israelis and Arabs reveals a marked contrast in substance, depth of knowledge and language. Reports on western leaders tend to be highly factual, even coldly professional in tone.[8] Similarly, even the "sanitized" (censored reports for public release in archives) biographies of Israeli leaders run to two or three densely packed, single-spaced pages and provide detailed information on their education, political development, professional careers and personal lives.[9]

In contrast, biographies of Arab leaders prepared by the State Department for use by the White House, including the president, are often highly superficial or even frivolous. The 1974 Fact Sheet on Saudi Arabia and King Faisal included material gleaned from *The Reader's Digest*, a magazine hardly known for its scholarly merit. While this report repeated highly sensationalized and unsubstantiated stories on Saudi profligacy and conspicuous consumption, it said almost nothing about Faisal's political orientation or philosophy.[10]

Other biographies described the Saudi Crown Prince (subsequently the King), members of the royal family and advisers as variously retaining "some of the appealing traits of ... Bedouin ancestry,"[11] having "appealing traits," or perhaps most ingenuously, as being "a Muslim."[12] Biographic sketches on Anwar Sadat similarly focused on his personal appearance, repeatedly describing him as a "dapper dresser with an omnipresent pipe."[13]

To some degree the inclusion of sartorial details and bland personality traits might indicate the work of junior staff, with little real knowledge, who add superfluous details in desperate attempts to fill out a meager page of information. On the other hand, that reports written in the 1970s on Saudi Arabia, a close ally of the United States for over 30 years, or of the much courted Anwar Sadat, should be riddled with facile generalizations indicates a failure, at the very highest levels of policy-making, to bridge the cultural divide. In the absence of balanced, objective information, experts and decision-makers seem likely to fall back on "default responses," bringing into play images and distortions they have assimilated, consciously or unconsciously, from the general cultural milieu.

Ignorance about Islam and Arab culture hampers the formulation of objective or effective foreign policy. When discussing the difficulty of developing a policy to deal with the 1979 hostage crisis in Iran, one official in the Carter White House bluntly admitted that "No one really understood Islam, all the crazy things were happening over there."[14]

Unsubstantiated hypotheses regarding Arab nations and leaders have also been posited during discussions between government officials and Israelis, who are scarcely neutral observers. In 1968, Walter Rostow observed, in a conversation with Yitzhak Rabin (then Ambassador Designate to the United States), that Nasser was obsessed with "the Arab-Israeli problem and Arab nationalism."[15] Rostow then opined that the Soviet Union would lose interest in Egypt when it had to deal with a leader "interested in more rational development."[16] Here, Rostow not only concluded that Nasser's policies were irrational (presumably because the U.S. did not like them), but also audaciously predicted Soviet behavior in the Middle East.

Conversely, policy papers routinely reflect positively on Israel and negatively on Arab states. Recommended reading lists are heavily slanted toward studies favorable to Israel. Summaries on the history of the Arab Israeli conflict likewise lack objectivity. Labels or "code words" used for specific actions or policies are often identical to those employed in the Israeli lexicon and by the U.S. media. Hence, reports routinely refer to the "Arab refugee problem," not the Palestinian refugees; the "non-Jewish population," not the Palestinians; or Israeli "retaliatory raids," not attacks into Jordan, while similar Arab attacks into Israel are labeled as "terrorism."[17]

By the 1980s high-ranking government officials, heavily committed to Israel, openly talked about a new generation of Jewish scholars and policy analysts that saw "no conflict between their Jewish identification and their sympathetic attitude toward Israel ... and ... their ability to fully serve the interest of the United States, nor should they."[18]

With many authors already predisposed to favor Israel, it is not surprising that government biographies on Israeli leaders tend to downplay their involvement in violent or terrorist activities against either the British during the Mandate era or against the Arabs. For example, a biographical sketch on Ariel Sharon described him as heading Unit 101, which engaged in nothing more than "retaliatory action versus terrorists."[19]

The terrorist activities of both the Irgun and Stern Gang, characterized as "a Jewish underground movement that operated in Palestine during the British mandate,"[20] and as a "preindependence, anti-British, Underground organ,"[21] similarly distort the historic reality.

The biographies of Israeli Prime Minister Menachim Begin, who led the Irgun adjudged by the British government to be a "terrorist" Jewish organization during the 1940s, so obfuscated the historic facts that George Ball, a former Under Secretary of State and adviser to several presidents, surmised that during the Camp David negotiations, Carter might not have "known of Begin's past [as leader of the Irgun] as Israeli government downplay it."[22] In this instance, Ball's supposition is highly unlikely, since it is well-known that Carter spent "hours and hours and hours" with Brzezinski, Vance and others to educate himself on foreign policy.[23] According to Carter's close advisers, "Camp David was a product of how thoroughly he understood all of the elements of the Middle Eastern problem down to the last comma and period."[24] Distorted or slanted reports and biographies are far more likely to have a damaging impact under presidents such as Ronald Reagan or George W. Bush, who are not widely read and who pay little attention to detail.

Similarly, reading lists for White House officials are often heavily slanted toward a pro-Israeli and anti-Arab stance. For example, prior to the 2003 U.S. invasion of Iraq, officials cited the heavily biased and anti-Arab book, *The Arab Mind* by Raphael Patai (New York: Charles Scribner's Sons, 1973) as the basis for their characterizations of Arabs and Islamic culture. Over 30 years old, Patai's descriptions of Arabs as being sex-obsessed and shame-driven would be openly ridiculed and correctly condemned as racist were they about any other ethnic or racial group.

Lobby efforts operate within the constraints of the U.S. political system and within the cultural attitudes of the society. Because the cultural backdrop in the United States compliments a pro-Zionist agenda, pro-Israeli organizations have the built-in advantage of playing before an audience that is generally favorably predisposed. Conversely, Arab, Iranian or Turkish supporters often face hostile audiences and must overcome these prevailing negative cultural images before they can even present their case.

The widely held and disseminated negative stereotyping of Arabs and Muslims has historically made foreign policy decisions, such as

U.S. military involvement in the Lebanon in 1958, the ongoing U.S. attacks on Iraq in the 1990s, the full scale invasion and occupation in 2003, and, more recently, demands from some quarters for attacks on a wide array of Arab and Muslim nations, easy to sell to the American public and to politicians as well. They also form the cultural backdrop that made the abuses against Arabs and Muslims in Abu Ghraib prison in Iraq and elsewhere possible, if not probable.[25] The dehumanization and open ridicule of Arab/Islamic culture extends from the highest echelons of government to the young enlisted soldiers, as well as to voters in U.S. elections.[26]

Ironically, this deeply embedded hostility to Arabs and Muslims within the American psyche has, on occasion, impeded presidents from adopting policies that ran counter to the prevailing climate of opinion. The political opposition to President Ford's policies regarding the Turkish invasion of Cyprus in 1974, or the difficulties in gaining Congressional approval for arms sales to Saudi Arabia, a loyal U.S. ally, is illustrative of the push–pull effects created by prevailing cultural attitudes. Obviously, lobbyists manipulate and utilize these images to further their own agendas. "Battling for the hearts and minds of the American elite has been the true subject of the Arab-Israeli war for Washington."[27] The following chapters describe the various techniques used by lobbyists, introduce the Greek American lobby in its struggle against the Turkish occupation of Cyprus and spotlight the performers on both sides of the divide – pro-Arab lobbyists and interest groups and Israeli and pro-Zionist groups.

4
Production Aspects:
Lobby Techniques and Finances

Operating within the constraints of the system, lobbyists and domestic pressure groups manipulate and utilize the prevailing cultural milieu, first to gain access to, and then to convince, policy-makers to adopt policies that are favorable to their specific agendas. Specifically, they want "a comfortable competitive advantage over other industries."[1] Professional lobbyists, based in Washington, and interest groups from across the nation all endeavor to influence foreign policy.

The latter, representing a multitude of ethnic groups and political viewpoints, are generally unpaid, volunteer organizations. Under U.S. law, a lobbyist is defined as an individual or organization whose job is to "influence the passing or defeat of legislation" and who receives money for that purpose.[2]

By the 1990s, there were over 80,000 registered lobbyists in Washington, most of whom concentrated on domestic issues. There is general agreement that lobbyists have major impacts on domestic legislation, Congressional votes and, through personal contacts and financial contributions, to political parties and individual politicians. The impact of lobbyists on foreign policy is less clear, although the prevailing wisdom holds that lobbyists have had less influence on foreign policy than on domestic issues. The impact of domestic pressure groups on foreign policy is similarly unclear, but as this study demonstrates, some groups (on specific issues, at different times) have had considerable clout and impact.

Just as the media in the United States do *not* set the agenda or have major impacts on foreign policy, but rather follow the lead of Washington, so too may lobbies serve to reinforce predetermined policies, particularly because, as previously noted, U.S. foreign policy is remarkably consistent under both Republican and Democratic administrations.[3]

Similarly, the agendas of individual lobbyists or pressure groups do not generally change from administration to administration. Indeed, it is not unusual for lobbyists or "experts" on the Middle East to work at different times for both Republicans and Democrats.

Although the approaches of various lobby groups may very slightly from administration to administration, their techniques and goals remain the same.

Paid lobbyists operate under a common set of rules that do not necessarily pertain to pressure or interest groups. Rules that lobbyists profess to live by include: tell the truth, only promise what you can produce, listen and work with government personnel and, most importantly, do not surprise politicians with unexpected proposals or demands. Lobbyists and pressure groups must *clearly* define their agendas and know the influential decision-makers. Access is essential. Lobbyists can sometimes be successful on the basis of a close, personal relationship with just one powerful senator or representative.[4] Just as the entire cast in an operatic performance must work together, so too must lobbyists build consensus among the various officials who make foreign policy.[5]

Lobbyists also agree that 80–90 percent of the issues are decided on the basis of politics, not merit.[6] This consideration is particularly crucial with regard to policies regarding Israel and the Palestinians. Finally, lobbyists and pressure groups can educate and provide information on specific issues to policy-makers, and sometimes to the general public. A lobbyist or pressure group may therefore be one of the few or sole sources of information on a given issue. This is particularly relevant for issues dealing with the Middle East, a region, as previously noted, that is widely misunderstood, misrepresented or unknown to the vast majority of Americans as well as to many politicians.

For example, the American Israel Public Affairs Committee (AIPAC), arguably the most effective lobbyist organization involved with the Middle East, regularly sends *Facts and Myths*, *Near East Report* and a host of other publications by pro-Israeli writers to White House officials and politicians. During the Carter administration, AIPAC sent the 1976 *Facts and Myths* to the White House with a covering letter that Carter would find it of interest since he might not know the "actual facts" of the 1948 war.

White House Officials also received Joan Peters' totally pro-Israeli "Report on Middle East Refugees" in which Peters made the astonishing allegation that Syria had 100 percent employment and therefore the "sensible arrangement"[7] would be for the Palestinian refugees to be resettled in Syria or elsewhere in the Arab world. Peters expanded on this theme in the widely discredited history of the Arab

Israeli conflict, *From Time Immemorial: The Origins of the Arab-Jewish Conflict over Palestine* (New York: Harper & Row, 1984).

On the pro-Arab side, the Saudi Arabian embassy sent Carter aide Hamilton Jordan the glossy anthology, *The Genius of Arab Civilization: Sources of the Renaissance*, John R. Hayes, ed. (New York: New York University Press, 1975) in the hope of providing a positive account of Arab contributions and achievements. In his thank you note, Jordan added a handwritten addendum that "Your beautiful gift has been a great help to me in understanding the history and culture of your people."[8]

However, pro-Israeli pressure groups are much more consistent and persistent in "information campaigns" to provide officials with publications that present the Israeli point of view. They devote considerable time, energy and money to depicting Israel in the most favorable terms. These groups view the conflict as a zero sum game in which there is a "fixed pie" whereby it is impossible for one party to the conflict to advance without hurting the other party. In zero sum games the pie is a fixed size. Hence Zionist lobbyists and interest groups have tended to believe that any gain for the Palestinians or the Arabs would mean a loss for Israel, as opposed to a positive sum game wherein the pie grows and a gain for the Palestinians would not necessarily mean a loss for Israel. Consequently, the Zionist lobby acts not only as an advocate for Israel, but also as an anti-Palestinian and Arab force. The Zionist lobby tends to oppose any U.S. rapprochement with the Arab world. Any sign that a president or administration might be moving away from a completely pro-Israeli stance or toward Palestinian and/or Arab positions is guaranteed to elicit a loud outcry from the Zionist lobby. Spokespersons for Israel in the United States frequently take a harder line than the Israelis themselves. For example, Vice President Walter Mondale under Jimmy Carter was described by one Carter appointee as "really 150% pro-Israel. He's more pro-Israel than Begin."[9]

Former President Reagan was described by Stuart Eizenstat, Carter's Assistant to the President for Domestic Affairs and an ardent Zionist supporter, as having a "particularly warm spot in his heart toward Israel, as did his Secretary of State George Shultz";[10] according to Eizenstat, the relationship between the U.S. and Israel "blossom[ed] into a strategic alliance"[11] under Reagan.

During performances singers use a variety of vocal techniques to give color and impact to their performances; so too do lobbyists and pressure groups have a set collection of techniques. Lobbyists and interest groups use a variety or combination of the same, quite simple, techniques to gain attention and support for their causes. These techniques can be divided into eight major categories.

LETTER/TELEPHONE/FAX/EMAIL CAMPAIGNS

These campaigns may be directed to the White House, other relevant branches of the government (Senate, House of Representatives), or a combination of all of the above. Although simple letters, unless written by individuals known to the White House or a high level politician, are generally ignored, the others usually elicit direct or indirect responses from the White House or Congressional representatives. In most instances White House personnel write and sign the responses. These pro forma responses are usually written in boilerplate language to the effect "The President thanks you for your interest in this matter." However, White House advisers occasionally recommend a direct presidential response to specific letters or communications. In addition, letters, calls or messages from well-known individuals or leaders of major organizations receive personal responses from presidents or high-ranking White House officials. Major letter/FAX/email or telephone campaigns tend to receive the most attention from new administrations that are anxious to gauge public opinion and support. During their first months in office, new presidents invariably announce they are reassessing Middle East policy. Letter campaigns have the most impact during this relatively short timeframe (three to four months). In their respective memoirs, *A Time to Heal* (1979) and *Keeping Faith* (1982), Presidents Ford and Carter both noted the concern expressed by domestic pressure groups over possible changes in Middle East policy.

During the Ford administration, the responses to the few letters advocating better relations with Arab governments and consideration of Palestinian rights typify White House reactions to such correspondence. Responses were generally directed through the office of the director of correspondence. For example, when the National Association of Arab-Americans (NAAA) official Edmond Howar wrote in opposition to the Israeli bombing of the Lebanon, the White House response was signed by Brent Scowcroft of the National Security Council and was phrased in a cordial, yet noncommittal vein, to the effect that Ford "welcomes your views."[12]

Administrations also keep close track of the numbers of responses and communications – on all issues – and tally positive and negative comments on specific policies.[13] The White House views these campaigns as bellwethers for gauging public opinion, not as the basis for forming foreign policy.

DIRECT, PERSONAL CONTACTS WITH THE PRESIDENT AND WHITE HOUSE OFFICIALS

Presidents try to maintain at least some personal contact with various lobbying groups. They meet with lobbyists on a fairly regular basis, or whenever a major policy decision is about to be or has been taken. As with letter writing campaigns, personal contacts are particularly crucial during the early weeks of reassessment. Thereafter, direct meetings generally occur *after* policies have been decided, or when there has been widespread public or political pressure from a specific group or organization to meet with the president or other top officials. The individual style of each president, as with conductors, is also a factor in determining the relative importance and frequency of personal meetings. Presidents Ford and Reagan both delegated enormous amounts of work to others. In the case of the Ford White House, Secretary of State Henry Kissinger, along with the National Security Council (NSC), exercised almost total control over the formation of foreign policy. Ford became involved primarily on the domestic front and, in particular, used his inside knowledge of Congress to persuade and gather support for what were often rather unpopular policies as, for example, the resumption of economic and military aid to Turkey after it invaded Cyprus in 1974. Other presidents, such as Nixon, have skillfully manipulated their media image to political advantage.[14] Subsequently, Reagan often gained public acceptance for his policies by using his acknowledged communication skills in the mass media.

In contrast, Carter was very much a hands-on president, particularly in the field of foreign policy. Showing considerable flexibility and willingness to change previously held opinions, Carter constantly solicited differing points of view by holding substantive discussions of foreign policy at weekly Friday morning breakfast meetings.[15] Close advisers observed that Carter usually turned papers around in 24 hours and that his work day was probably double that of President Reagan.

Some presidents, such as Truman and Ford, also had close personal friendships with individuals who had extensive interests in Middle East, particularly with Israel. Truman's friend, Eddie Jacobson, and

Ford's friend, Max Fisher, both argued and pushed for the United States to support Israel.[16]

During his presidency, Ford met with Max Fisher over 50 times.[17] Fisher, a well-known businessman from Michigan, Ford's home state, was an outspoken supporter of Israel as well as a leading fund-raiser for the Republican party. While not all of these meetings involved issues relating to the Middle East, Fisher was regularly consulted on policies regarding Israel and the Jewish American community. Fisher helped to arrange and lead delegations of Jewish Americans to the White House for special briefings and also frequently met with key White House officials before and after his regular trips to Israel.

Interestingly, the Ford administration not only listened to what Fisher had to say, but also used his good offices to send "behind the scenes" messages to the Israelis. Before Fisher's trip to Israel in the summer of 1976, the NSC suggested that Fisher reassure the Israelis as to Ford's policies and keep them informed as to public opinion in the United States. Fisher also acted as an intermediary between Israeli Labor party leaders and the White House.[18]

In election years, the White House works diligently to keep in touch with domestic/lobby interest groups. White House appointees are delegated to deal directly with designated organizations and groups. During the 1976 campaign Myron Kuropas, Special Assistant for Ethnic Affairs, worked to gain support for Ford among Americans of Polish, Hungarian, Slovenian and other (mostly European) ethnic groups. As the 1980 Presidential campaign heated up, Alfred Moses was brought in by Carter as a special adviser to act as a liaison specifically with the Jewish community. Moses viewed the position as a means not only of improving communications between the Jewish community and Carter, but as an opportunity to influence foreign policy.[19]

No Arab American has ever had such close personal contacts with a president or, indeed, even with ranking White House officials. However, as the Fisher case demonstrates, personal contacts are two-way streets. The conductor/president interacts with the soloist/friend/lobbyist in a give and take process. Presidents can also use a friend's personal contacts to communicate or to sell specific foreign policy decisions to lobbyists and organizations, rather than the other way around. As the Fisher case illustrates, presidents may also use personal friends to carry communications to foreign governments or opinion-makers in foreign nations.

PERSONAL CONTACTS WITH ELECTED OFFICIALS AND THEIR AIDES

Paid lobbyists and pressure groups devote considerable energy to maintaining close contact with a wide range of government officials. Officials from the president on-down-the-line are consistently asked to make appearances at conferences, to dedicate buildings, to give speeches and to send messages of support or recognition. Family members, including wives and children, are also invited to dinners, teas and social events held by organizations/groups. On the highest levels, such requests are carefully vetted by the White House staff or individual congressional aides. The staff usually determines whether the request is appropriate, what political value the event has, or whether the appearance might cause some sort of diplomatic or political backlash.

For example, until the late 1990s, requests for appearances that would seem to give the U.S. stamp of approval to Israeli control over the West Bank were consistently rejected, but meetings with Palestinians were also usually denied. Ford was advised not to meet with Elias Freij, mayor of Bethlehem, on the grounds that "it would not be appropriate for the President to meet with a citizen of the West Bank."[20]

The paucity of pressure by or contact with individual Arab Americans, or other citizens interested in Palestinian or Arab issues, has severely limited their information effort within top government offices and in both the House and Senate. Owing to the steady pressure by pro-Israeli groups, politicians and advisers have been reluctant to deal openly and/or directly with Arabs or Arab Americans, even those who have been "courted" by the United States. Even a meeting between Ford and a high-ranking delegation of visiting Egyptian Parliamentarians caused considerable debate among the staff. When the Egyptians arrived in spring 1975, Anwar Sadat had met with 150 members of the U.S. Congress in the preceding four months. In the face of the reluctance to meet directly with the Egyptians, U.S. Ambassador Herman Eilts exerted considerable pressure by emphasizing that the U.S. had worked hard to make friends with Sadat. Robert Oakley, the NSC Near East and South Asia Area Director, argued that although some Israelis might criticize Ford, the President had "a good record of meeting Israelis."[21] Ford did meet with the Egyptian delegation, the first such meeting since 1967, but to assure a quid pro quo, a similar delegation of Israeli Parliamentarians, visiting Washington at the invitation of the Speaker of the House, Carl Albert, and Senator Mike Mansfield, subsequently also met with Ford. That the Israeli delegation had been invited to Washington by top elected officials is just one example of the power of Zionist pressure groups and their close relationship with many politicians in Washington.

In the realm of pressure politics, the Israelis and pro-Israeli groups hold the advantage with far better and easier access to decision-makers. Relationships with junior officials or aides, cultivated over many years, also often reap benefits as young professionals become senior officials in key decision-making positions. With long term planning and foresight, pro-Zionist groups have been particularly successful in developing and maintaining contacts and personal relationships with junior officials at local and state levels, as well as in Washington.

NATIONAL ORGANIZATIONS/SPECIAL INTEREST GROUPS

Special interest groups use a wide variety of techniques to exert direct pressure on the White House. National organizations, composed of a wide variety of individuals and groups, work to influence U.S. Middle East policies. A multitude of Jewish American organizations have been extremely active in political and social realms for many decades. These organizations keep the White House and politicians informed of their many activities and programs. The Anti-Defamation League (ADL), American Israel Public Affairs Committee (AIPAC), Leaders of National Jewish Organizations and the Conference of American Rabbis are among the most active and visible of pro-Zionist groups which actively seeking the support and attention of U.S. policy makers.[22]

Presidents regularly appoint liaisons to meet with domestic pressure groups as well as to provide information on their activities and to follow their publications. When organizations hold national conventions or publish materials thought to be of political or international importance, staff members pass on pertinent information, write memos regarding the organizations and, by a variety of other means, communicate directly with the president and others in the White House and government offices.

As a result of their size, efficient organization and personal contacts with members of the White House staff, Jewish American groups and pro-Israeli lobbyists have no difficulty in gaining direct access to high-level officials, including the president. Zionist lobbyists also use their knowledge of and friendships with Israeli leaders to gain easy access to high level U.S. officials and the mainstream media. Contacts in Israel can also be instrumental in securing consulting jobs for key government agencies.[23] The extraordinarily close U.S. Israel relationship, which in part evolved owing to the work and success of Zionist lobbyists and organizations that move easily from America to Israel and back again, has been characterized by George Ball, former Under Secretary of State and noted diplomat, as the "Passionate Attachment."[24]

Presidents regularly meet with the leaders of national organizations to hear their opinions and, more importantly, to explain and gather support for their programs and policies. When matters of foreign policy are involved, both the State Department and particularly the National Security Council, view these meetings either as possible obstructions to the implementation of predetermined policies or as political necessities. The National Security Council often rejects or delays meetings with organizations or groups on the basis of national security or foreign policy considerations. At times, direct political intervention, particularly from ranking members of Congress who have vested political interests in securing meetings with the president for their constituents, is necessary to override NSC decisions. For example, under the Ford administration requests for meetings with leaders from ethnic Baltic communities were rejected until Ed Derwinski, a personal friend of the president and director of the nationalities division of the Republican National Committee, intervened directly.[25]

In contrast to other domestic pressure groups, members of Jewish American organizations have direct channels to the president through specific liaison staff officers working in the White House. The Johnson administration was the first to designate an "adviser" or an "advocate" for specific interest groups; under the Ford administration the liaisons were placed under one umbrella.[26] Myron Kuropas was hired as the liaison for "Ethnics;" in this capacity he identified about 100 major groups that comprised approximately 60–80 million ethnic Americans. Neither Arab nor Jewish groups were placed under this rubric. Individuals within the White House were designated to deal specifically with Jewish American groups; thus staff loyalty may be to specific groups rather than to general presidential policy. No staff member deals solely with the concerns of Arab, Turkish or Iranian Americans. Crucially, the concerns of these Middle Eastern peoples are treated as matters of foreign policy, not domestic policy.

The existence of staff offices dealing directly with the Jewish community clearly demonstrates its domestic political clout. Liaisons for the Jewish American groups are often appointed on the basis of their close personal and professional experience with the Jewish community. They find it easy to arrange direct meetings with the president and other high-ranking officials. The existence of specific White House liaisons for Jewish Americans ensures that Israeli interests will be presented by officials with direct access to the president, Secretary of State and National Security Council. Conversely, it also ensures that Israel and its supporters are appraised of possible shifts or changes in U.S. policy in the Middle East.

Meetings of Jewish American groups with the president have long been recognized as a regular and necessary feature of domestic politics. Presidential staffs carefully orchestrate all meetings, determining not only a rigid time schedule but precisely when and if the president will appear and if there will be a "photo opportunity."

PRESSURE ON CONGRESS, STATE AND LOCAL GOVERNMENTS

Pressure from Congress, state and local governments also influences presidential policies. When policies involving the Middle East are involved, Congressional and state government pressure is almost always favorable to Israel. Former Senator Paul Findley and others have described the impact of pro-Israeli lobbyists on the domestic political scene.[27]

Presidents with extensive experience in Congress and Washington undoubtedly have the edge in obtaining Congressional support for their domestic programs and foreign policies. President Ford came to office with decades of experience in national government and was personally acquainted with many members of Congress. Consequently, although the Democrats retained a majority in both the House and Senate, Ford was able to use his influence to secure Congressional votes. In contrast, Carter and Clinton, with no experience in Washington but with a Democratic Congress, were unable to "call home" old political favors to secure Congressional votes.

Members of Congress can also elevate levels of concern by making public statements or issuing collective public letters on specific policies. In the instances of Cyprus and the anti-Arab Boycott, described in subsequent chapters, they can also call for hearings of specific issues, launch investigations and, of course, they can draw up bills for Congressional approval into law. However, historically, in areas of substantive importance to U.S. Middle East policy, Congress generally has exercised little influence. Direct Congressional involvement in decisions as far ranging as the Geneva conference or Madrid, Camp David, the Iran–Iraq War, sanctions versus Iraq, Oslo, the Gulf Wars, the 2003 invasion of Iraq and direct involvement in the Israeli Palestinian peace process has been minimal.[28]

On the other hand, Congress retains enormous power in two major areas: appropriations of foreign aid and arms sales. It is self-evident that Israel enjoys the overwhelming advantage in securing Congressional support for money and arms. In moving toward closer relations with Arab nations or in dealing with the many permutations of the Arab Israeli conflict, presidents must take into account the substantial support Israel enjoys in Congress. As will be demonstrated, policies that could be construed as harmful to Israeli interests, or as favoring the Arabs, cause vocal and vociferous opposition from both Democrats and Republicans in Congress. Political retribution soon follows.

Presidents are particularly vulnerable to political pressures in election years. Because first term presidents enter office already running for a second term, each must frame his foreign policy during the first four years in office within the constraints of domestic political considerations. Presidents have modified or delayed shifts in Middle Eat policy because of their candidacy for second terms. Had he been elected to a second term, Carter would have pursued the unresolved portions of the Camp David agreement with "tremendous vigor."[29] After leaving office, Carter publicly and correctly stated that he feared Prime Minister Begin had decided to ignore Camp David and would continue to confiscate property and land in the West Bank. Carter believed that some Arabs were ready to negotiate but were waiting for signs that Israel would do so in good faith. On this basis he anticipated that in his second term he could push through agreements involving Palestinian rights without the "political constraints ... of a first term president in these areas."[30]

PUBLICITY CAMPAIGNS TO GAIN POPULAR SUPPORT

Massive media campaigns encourage citizens to exert pressure on their political representatives and to vote for or against politicians who support or fail to support specific policies. Media blitzes on specific issues popularize specific agendas and garner public support. This aspect of the lobby effort has been noted in the previous chapter on the media and therefore needs no further explanation.

PRESSURE FOR LEGISLATION ON SPECIFIC ISSUES
AT CONGRESS, STATE AND LOCAL LEVELS

Lobbyists and interest groups also pressure individual congressional representatives and senators to support specific legislation. Through Political Action Committees (PACs), groups with specific foreign policy agendas often give financial support to political campaigns and individual politicians. As will be seen with pro-Israeli PACs, they can also funnel money to candidates running against incumbents who have taken stances contrary to the Zionist lobby. These donations can be on local, regional or national levels.

These techniques are employed within the context of the larger American political system. Successful lobbyists utilize the strengths and weaknesses of the system to gain support and, ultimately, the acceptance and adoption of their particular programs by the U.S. government. But no opera production or lobby campaign can be launched without financial backing.

THE ANGELS OR FINANCIAL BACKERS

In the world of opera, the case of Alberto Vilar is instructive. Over the past 20 years, Vilar has donated over $150 million to opera and the arts. While his love and commitment to the world of opera cannot be denied, Vilar also expects some return on his investments. In his own words, "Let me crack the code of philanthropy for you: You Must Appreciate. Human beings like to hear the word Thank You. When you give $50 million the least people can do is to say Thank You."[31]

Lobbyists also expect a "thank you" in the form of political support for their causes. Obviously, mounting an operatic production or lobby campaign takes financial backing in order to pay personnel, for publicity and to "wine and dine" the prospective target audience. In the political arena, financial support frequently takes the form of campaign money for individuals running for political office.

A myriad of constantly changing federal laws govern campaign fundraising and lobbyists must work within these regulations. Over the past three decades PACs have been one of the most effective ways for individuals and groups to help politicians who support their causes get elected. [32] Individual pro-Arab and pro-Israeli pressure groups will be described in the following two chapters. Here the focus is on the laws governing financial donations or those paid to lobby or represent specific foreign nations or causes.

Within the realm of fund-raising, it is crucial to differentiate between "hard money" and "soft money." Hard money is funds raised for campaign expenses for federal positions by political parties or candidates. Under U.S. laws an individual can only give $2,000 to a candidate for each election and no more than $25,000 to a national party committee; individuals can give no more than $57,500 per year to political parties.[33] Soft money is given by individuals, corporations and unions. Under new 2003 laws this money is no longer legal. Most soft money used to come from corporations, unions or a few wealthy individuals. Ironically, the Democrats, who pushed for the new legislation to outlaw soft money, are the ones most affected by the new ban since they traditionally received more large donations from labor unions.

The new regulations promise to be a boon for special interest groups as they are now permitted to receive large donations from individuals and to spend the money on ads, turning out voters or providing information blitzes favoring candidates that support their causes. In other words, "People with big networks of friends and associates who can 'bundle' contributions for the parties and candidates are the new kings of the system."[34]

With a long tradition of "political philanthropy" and well-organized and financially sound lobby organizations, the Zionists now clearly have an even greater advantage in securing political support for their agenda in the Middle East. Arabs and Arab Americans are relative newcomers to the process of giving money to political parties or candidates. To make matters worse, politicians, fearing a political backlash from pro-Israeli forces, have shown a marked reluctance to accept support from Arab American groups.[35] Candidates as diverse as George McGovern, Walter Mondale, and mayor of Philadelphia, Wilson Goode, have all refused or returned donations from Arab Americans. More recently, mayor "Rudi" Giuliani of New York City returned a $10 million donation from Saudi prince Walid bin Talal for the World Trade Center relief fund after the 9/11 terrorist attacks. The mayor was widely praised for his refusal to accept "Arab" money. Thus Arabs or Arab Americans often find their attempts to enter the political process through "political philanthropy" thwarted at national, state, and local levels.

When Cyprus was invaded by Turkish troops in 1974, Greek Americans utilized all of the above techniques to mount a successful campaign forcing the U.S. government to ban further arms sales to Turkey, in spite of strong White House and Pentagon opposition. The subsequent analysis of Greek American efforts offers an interesting comparison without the emotive overtones of the Arab Israeli question and serves as an overture to other lobby efforts on behalf of special interest groups concerned with the Middle East.

5
An Overture: The Case of Cyprus

A glance at the map shows why Cyprus has been a flashpoint of contention for thousands of years. As they say in the real estate business, it is all about "location, location, location." Situated in the southeastern corner of the Mediterranean, Cyprus is within the competing spheres of interest of Turkey, the Arab nations, Greece and Israel. During the Cold War, the island also served as a strategic imperative for the West. In the contemporary era, Cyprus has been an important military outpost for Great Britain and, by extension, the United States.

Ruled as a British Crown Colony from 1925, Cyprus achieved independence in 1960 following a brutal struggle between Greek Cypriots and British forces. Fearing the Greek desire for Enosis (union with Greece) ethnic Turkish Cypriots tended to side with Britain, which often favored the Turkish minority as a counterweight to Greek Cypriot demands. Independent Cyprus was governed on a proportional basis between the two communities with Great Britain retaining two military Sovereign Base Areas in perpetuity. A treaty of guarantee in 1960 allowed Great Britain, Greece or Turkey to act jointly or independently to fight any threat to the constitution. Archbishop Makarios was elected the first president of the independent state. His policy of non-alignment annoyed Washington where he was frequently referred to as the "Red Bishop." Makarios sought to internationalize the Cyprus issue to avoid either Greek or Turkish interference in the affairs of the island. Radicals on both sides of the ethnic divide opposed Makarios' independent line and, when inter-communal tensions erupted into open violence, over 6,000 U.N. troops were sent in to enforce the fragile ceasefire in 1964.

In July 1974 a coup devised by the military junta in Greece, and implemented by radical Greek Nationalists from the Cypriot National Guard, moved to overthrow President Makarios who narrowly escaped an assassination attempt. He fled to London where he mounted an international campaign to restore Cypriot independence. Five days after the coup, Turkey invoked the 1960 Treaty of Guarantee and invaded the island, quickly occupying almost 40 percent of the land. An estimated 160,000 to 200,000 Greek Cypriots fled the newly occupied Turkish territory while 60,000–65,000 Turkish Cypriots fled the Greek dominated areas.[1] The U.N. General Assembly unanimously called for all states to respect the territorial integrity and independence of Cyprus and Makarios resumed his presidency – a position he held until his death in 1977. United Nations peacekeepers were stationed along the "green line" dividing the two sides. But Turkey refused to withdraw its forces and in the ensuing years exacerbated the problem by moving in over 40,000 settlers from the Anatolian peninsula. Turkey also granted Turkish army officers Greek-owned land as rewards for services rendered. In 1975 the Turkish Cypriot nationalist leader, Rauf Denktash, proclaimed the independence of the Turkish Federated State of Cyprus (changed to the Turkish Republic of North Cyprus (TRNC), in 1983). Turkey was the only state to recognize the TRNC which was effectively isolated from the international community. Despite protracted negotiations, the two sides failed to resolve their differences and the island remained divided even after the South joined the E.U. in 2004.[2]

Although the international community overwhelmingly condemned the Turkish invasion, President Ford and Kissinger viewed the crisis from a Cold War perspective and were primarily concerned that Turkey should remain a close NATO ally and military bastion against possible Soviet expansion. By emphasizing the Greek and Turkish aspects of the crisis, the administration relegated Cyprus to a subordinate role.

Although responses to the crisis from the White House were markedly low-key, the invasion provoked a storm of protests from Greek Americans who demanded that Washington condemn the invasion and force the Turks to withdraw their troops. Historically Greek American organizations had focused on domestic issues as they pertained to their constituency in the United States, not on lobbying for Greece or Cyprus. But the Turkish aggression in Cyprus enraged and mobilized Greek Americans. The Greek lobby enjoyed a number of advantages. They both knew and cared about the issue and they could, and did, call upon built-in cultural bias favorable to the Greeks and hostile to the Turks.

The absence of any pro-Turkish ethnic lobbying efforts enabled Greek Americans to dominate public debates. The pro-Greek lobby framed effective arguments around the moral justice of the Greek Cypriot cause. Through Orthodox churches, ethnic clubs, the American Hellenic Educational Progressive Association (AHEPA), the United Hellenic American Congress (UHAC) and the American

Hellenic Institute (AHI, the only registered Greek lobby), Greek Americans orchestrated media and letter campaigns and personal visits to Congressmen, Senators and White House officials. They forcefully and effectively argued the case for Greek Cypriots against the Turkish occupation. When Greek Americans demonstrated outside the White House, Alexander Haig very reluctantly met with four Greek American representatives from the demonstration to discuss the Cypriot problem. Such high-profile demonstrations are most effective as lobby techniques when they attract favorable media coverage, thereby drawing the attention of the American public to the cause. They can, however, backfire if media coverage shows the demonstrators in an unfavorable, violent, or "anti-American" light.

Recognizing the moral issues as well as the political advantages to be gained by supporting Greek Americans, several key Congressmen (led by Senator Eagleton and Representatives Rosenthal and du Pont) submitted bills in the Senate and House to ban any monies for military assistance to Turkey.[3] The majority of Congress saw this as a cause in which they could adopt the moral high ground. The ban was a relatively free, feel-good opportunity and quickly garnered a majority in Congress. Dismayed by the potential damage to U.S. Turkish relations, President Ford characterized the Congressional initiative as interference "with the President's right to manage foreign policy."[4] This response was in noted contrast to the muted presidential reactions to similar Congressional initiatives on behalf of Israel.

Initially, White House aides minimized the effectiveness of the Greek lobby by stressing that "the Greeks are not like the Israelies [sic] in that they are not organized into economic and social power houses."[5] Having enjoyed warm relations with many ethnic Greek organizations, Ford was taken aback by the vehemence of the opposition to his stance on the Cypriot issue (as he was with the Zionist lobby's opposition to his "reassessment" of the Arab Israeli conflict).[6] He announced that he was "deeply disappointed" by the Congressional action while Kissinger called it "tragic." Ford vetoed the bill to ban arms sales to Turkey, but after the House had overridden his veto a second time, he grudgingly signed a third compromise appropriations bill over Kissinger's strenuous objections in December.[7] The compromise bills temporarily postponed the ban until February 1975, providing that Turkey honored the ceasefire and did not increase its troops stationed in northern Cyprus. Ford warned that "whatever we can still do to assist in resolving the Cyprus dispute will be done. But if we fail despite our best efforts, those in congress who overrode the congressional leadership must bear the full responsibility for that failure."[8]

After the embargo went into effect, Ford moved, not to placate the Greeks, but to lobby Congress for the repeal of the arms ban. In bipartisan leadership meetings, Ford used his considerable political acumen and personal friendships to press the Turkish case. He stressed that the embargo undermined Turkish confidence in the U.S. and that it threatened U.S. security interests because the Turkish government had warned that it might close down NATO and U.S. military bases on its territory. The Pentagon also rallied veteran groups to support arms sales to Turkey.

The Senate responded favorably and passed a bill calling for a partial lifting of the embargo in May. The new bill provided for purchases of arms on the commercial market, credits for NATO and the shipping of arms purchased prior to the embargo. Ford now had the job of selling the Senate bill to the House. But the chorus from Congress had refrains like "We need something to quiet the Greek community"; "Turks should take action ... like take home troops or machinery"; "the Turkish statement must be clear as to their prospective actions."[9] Some also expressed their mistrust of Kissinger who had reportedly told the Turkish government "Don't worry about Congress. We will find a way to turn Congress around."[10]

Ford dropped his normally "hands off" posture and intensified his own lobbying efforts by holding extensive meetings with hundreds of representatives. He also met with members of AHEPA to tell them that the anti-Turkish legislation jeopardized U.S. foreign interests and did not improve the likelihood of a resolution of the Cyprus issue. In the following months, Ford tried to diffuse Greek opposition by meeting with key community leaders, including the editor of the Boston based *Hellenic Chronicle*, a widely distributed journal aimed at the Greek communities.[11] In these meetings Ford cajoled and flattered Greek American leaders, doing his utmost to convince them to pressure their constituency into dropping their support for the arms embargo against Turkey.

The White House also sent out "factual" information giving its point of view on arms limitations to Turkey to key editorial writers from around the nation. White House efforts paid off when a few columnists wrote in favor of resuming arms sales to Turkey and criticized the Greek lobby for its "relentless" campaign that harmed U.S. foreign policy interests.[12] Similar allegations have been consistently and noticeably absent in opinion or op-ed pieces about the Zionist lobby's efforts on behalf of Israel and its possible damage to larger U.S. policy interests.

By early summer it appeared that Ford's efforts had paid off and that a compromise to reinstate aid to Turkey had been reached. The compromise provided for reopening the pipeline for arms that Turkey had previously purchased and allowed Turkey to make cash sales in the military foreign sales program. Under this compromise the president was to report to Congress every 60 days regarding "the progress of the sales and the progress, of course, of settling the Cyprus dispute."[13] Although the compromise fell far short of Ford's desire for a complete resumption of sales, and in spite of his best efforts, the Democratic Congress voted 206–223 not to lift the embargo on 24 July.

Turkey promptly retaliated by curtailing U.S. activities at joint bases the very next day. This led to the take over of 24 American military bases in Turkey. In a rare instance of direct, extensive involvement in foreign policy issues, Ford personally, and by hand, rewrote his statement on the Turkish decision. He placed the blame directly on Congress, urging the House to reconsider its "refusal to restore U.S. assistance to Turkey. Prompt affirmative actions by the House of Representatives is essential to the vital national defense interests of our country."[14] It was so unusual for Ford to mark up a policy statement that Ron Nessen wrote at the bottom of the page, "A collectors item! Please file."

But the White House kept up the pressure just as the Greek American lobby became less vociferous and active. In bargaining with the Black caucus Ford offered to take stronger stands on narcotic control in exchange for their votes to lift the arms embargo.[15] When Israel made it clear that it was "unhappy with Congressional action,"[16] the administration also attempted to rally the Zionist lobby to its side. This is an interesting intersection of the administration working with the pro-Zionist lobby to gain support on a separate, albeit regional, issue.

However, in October the House once again refused to lift the embargo. Ford angrily responded that the decision "will imperil our relationships with our Turkish friends and weaken us in the crucial Eastern Mediterranean ... Thus, I call upon the Senate to accept the original conference report ... And I ask the House of Representatives to reconsider its hasty act."[17] Ford then vetoed the continuing resolution stressing the need for bipartisan support in the best interests of U.S. foreign policy. Although he failed to secure the total lifting of the embargo, subsequent language allowed for greater "flexibility" regarding arms sales. Pursuant to Public Laws 94–104 Ford then began to submit progress reports on the Cyprus question every 60 days; these soon had a boilerplate format in which the administration assured Congress that it was attempting to get both sides (Turks and Greeks) to resolve the problem. However, in spite of the so-called "best efforts" of the United States the Turkish occupation continued and the island remains divided over 30 years later.

During the 1976 election campaign, Carter criticized Ford's pro-Turkish stance and argued that he, unlike Ford, would support human rights and the law. But once in office Carter, too, shifted toward a more pro-Turkish policy. Cyprus was not at the top of Carter's foreign policy agenda. (In his presidential memoir, *Keeping Faith*, he mentioned Turkey only in the context of the hostage crisis in Iran and its relations with Greece;[18] while Ford in *A Time to Heal: The Autobiography of Gerald R. Ford* raised the issue in five separate instances.[19]) However, Carter did lobby Congress to lift the embargo. Carter's shift away from his opposition to the Turkish occupation and his campaign statements regarding human rights in the context of the Greek Cypriot issue, was a disappointment to Greek Americans. But their rather perfunctory letter campaign was discounted by the White House.[20] As Greek American lobby efforts on behalf of Cyprus diminished, the Democratic Congress moved to reestablish closer military relations with Turkey, voting to lift the embargo in August 1978.

The Cyprus case demonstrates how an ethnic lobby effort, based on a moral cause for which the public already has engrained sympathies, can effectively counter or obstruct the foreign policy agenda of the White House and Pentagon. It also clearly demonstrates how the White House sees foreign policy as its exclusive purview and resents any attempts by Congress to upstage it. Following the successful Congressional opposition to White House policy on Cyprus and Turkey, one expert noted that,

> Now that they [Members of Congress] have gotten away with this, … they are going to try to intervene in every foreign policy issue you can think of – Israel, Panama, you name it. Some of them would like to set foreign policy from Capitol Hill. It's all part of the mood up there, with a lot of politics thrown in.[21]

The same attitudes that in the past had been instrumental in gaining public support were, in this instance, used to thwart White House policies. Importantly, Turkey exercised its strategic advantage and made the U.S. and NATO "pay" for hostile Congressional actions by shutting down or threatening to shut down western military bases in the Anatolian peninsula. As will be seen, Arab governments have not moved in similar strategic fashions when Washington ignored or rejected their interests regarding the Arab Israeli conflict or the Arab Boycott. In addition, Greek Americans, in contrast to the Zionist lobby, were unable or unwilling to maintain sustained, concerted pressure on Congress and the White House, nor did they build firm, long-lasting coalitions that would help to ensure that their foreign policy concerns would be supported by constantly shifting administrations over the long term. Finally, the case of Cyprus demonstrates that the White House can and will challenge ethnic lobbies and Congress on matters of foreign policy if it views key national interests to be at stake or if the domestic, political "payback" is not too high.

6
The Cast: Pro-Arab Lobbyists and Interest Groups

Singers are categorized according to their vocal ranges: sopranos, tenors, baritones; so too may the diverse cast of pro-Arab lobbyists and organizations be classified into several main categories.

ARAB GOVERNMENTS AND EMBASSIES

First, Arab governments, through their direct contacts and embassies in Washington, attempt to influence American foreign policy; however, their failure to coordinate lobbying efforts has hindered their overall effectiveness. Nor have Arab leaders always understood the dynamics of the U.S. political system. In the decades immediately following World War II, many Arab officials thought that lobbying was illegal and that all efforts should be directed solely through diplomatic channels.

In the 1950s, Nasser actually had to ask an aide, who had lived in the United States, "What is a lobby?" He also asked for a definition of "picket lines." Neither term existed in Arabic in the manner applied to U.S. politics. Although Egypt – in contrast to many other Arab states – had a well-established Foreign Service, it did not have a full-time lobbyist in Washington until the 1970s.[1]

Oil producing nations, particularly Saudi Arabia, viewed ARAMCO (Arabian American Oil Company) and other petroleum corporations as the appropriate intermediaries through which to communicate their views and desires to Washington. Others believed that the CIA had the major role in making foreign policy. Self-interest led petroleum companies, the CIA and some private lobbyists to perpetuate these mistaken beliefs. When many Third World nations realized the complexities of the U.S. system, they gave up trying to influence policy and went home, or they hired professional lobbyists to do the job. Thus, in the past, some Arab governments have paid huge amounts to U.S. based public relations firms and professional lobbyists to design publicity campaigns or to influence politicians. These efforts have sometimes been extremely clumsy or, in some instances, outright failures. In the wake of the 1990 Iraqi invasion, Kuwait hired the lobbying firm Hill and Knowlton to publicize Iraqi atrocities, but several of their more egregious claims were quickly proven to be fabrications, thereby causing embarrassment and doing more harm than good. By the 1990s, a number of Arab states had hired full-time or part-time lobbyists; however, they did not usually coordinate their efforts and often even worked at cross-purposes with one another. This obviously limited or negated the effectiveness of all their efforts.

Many Third World leaders, Arabs included, also believed that access to the top man – in this case the president – was the only effective way to influence policy. Generally, nations from the Global South have lacked direct access to the White House or other top-level government bureaus. A few ambassadors have been the exceptions to this rule. During the 1970s, Ardeshir Zahedi, the Iranian ambassador, was known for his direct lines of communication to the White House, as well as for his often criticized "over the top" embassy parties and lavish gift-giving. President Carter even used Zahedi as a go-between with the Shah in the months prior to the collapse of the monarchy.[2]

From the 1970s, the Saudi royal family also successfully established close personal relations with presidents and top U.S. officials. Prince Fahd officially visited Washington in 1974 and helped to establish the U.S. Saudi Joint Commission on Economic Cooperation. Subsequent cooperative agreements followed. The Egyptians developed similar joint agencies that aimed to foster trade and investment in 1990s. Fahd, then Crown Prince, met with Carter and Vance in 1977 in Washington and again with Carter in 1978 in Riyadh. From the 1990s to the present, Prince Bandar bin Sultan bin Abdulaziz al-Saud, the Saudi ambassador to the U.S., has had good access to the White House and apparently enjoys warm personal relations with both Bush senior and George W. Bush. With over 20 years service in the capital, Bandar is now dean of the Washington diplomatic corps. Perhaps not coincidently, the representatives with the benefit of easy access are from regimes closely tied or heavily dependant on the United States. They were also two of the least democratic and most repressive governments in the entire Middle East.

The PLO also has a full time spokesman in Washington but the organization has failed to frame its publicity campaigns or presentations in terms or images that are resonant with the U.S. public. The Institute of Palestine Studies publishes books and studies to keep Palestinian history and culture alive, but their publications reach very limited audiences. More recently, a small group of Arab Americans organized The American Task Force on Palestine (ATFP) to push Palestinian causes in Washington and to send spokespersons to testify before Congress to explain Palestinian positions.

LEAGUE OF ARAB STATES

The League of Arab states would seem to be the appropriate organization to spearhead Arab lobby efforts, but it too has failed to frame its campaigns in terms that would capture the imagination or support of American audiences. In some measure this is due to widespread ignorance in the Arab world about the U.S. political system and the dynamics that drive public opinion. This is a direct result of the failure to study U.S. history or culture and is in notable contrast to Israel. From its inception, Israel recognized the importance of understanding and working within the U.S. system and has devoted considerable monetary and intellectual resources to maintain institutes that study the role of public opinion polls, media, politics and government in the United States. Israel also supports centers for the study of the Arab world and the Arabic language. In contrast, Arab governments have been reluctant or even hostile to the study of Israel and Hebrew.

Israeli investments in "knowing your enemy" have paid off and Arab causes have suffered proportionately. Edward Said addressed the Arab lack of knowledge in a 2001 interview, noting:

> ... since Israel was established [over 50 years ago], the Israelis and their supporters in this country have put untold amounts of effort and money into propaganda, in regards to which not one single Arab regime or even the [Palestine Liberation Organization] has understood the power of the media and propaganda in this country. And that, I think, is a major crime of responsibility for every Arab leader and intellectual who considers himself to be serious. We still have no understanding of the power of the media and what you might call the "cultural work" of civil society ... And Israel has just announced another $100 million campaign to improve its image. And we do nothing.[3]

In 2000, the University of Jordan established the first degree program in American Studies in the Arab world and in 2003 the American University of Beirut announced the creation of a Center for American Studies underwritten by a $5.2 million donation from Saudi Prince Alwaleed bin Talal Abdulaziz al-Saud. These are steps in the right direction, but Israel has a 50-year head start.

The efforts of the Arab League have also been hindered by its failure to coordinate long-term, clear-cut policies.[4] Since 1967 the League has discussed formulating a "strategy" for the "information war." By 1984 (17 years later!) it had yet to do so.[5] For over a decade, Dr. Clovis Maksoud, ambassador and permanent observer of the League of Arab States to the U.N. and chief representative in the United States, was an energetic and effective spokesperson. A brilliant orator, Maksoud pursued the Arab information effort vigorously in 1980s and 1990s, making hundreds of public appearances in 1983 alone.[6] During the 1980s, the League also published *Arab Perspectives*, a monthly magazine with a fairly lively mix of articles on the Arab world and its relations with the international community.

But the Gulf War reinforced the disarray within both the Arab League and Arab diplomatic services. Occasionally, Arab ambassadors succeeded in coordinating efforts around a specific issue, for example, the massacre by an Israeli settler of Palestinians praying at the main mosque in Hebron in 1994 or the Israeli attack on Qana in southern Lebanon in 1999. On the other hand, in 2003/04 some Arab American expatriates from Lebanon and Syria even joined the chorus – led by neo-conservatives and Zionist lobby groups – supporting the Syrian Accountability Act and the imposition of U.S. economic sanctions on Syria. Thus Arab regimes and some Arab Americans often operate independently from one another. Rather than singing in unison or even in harmony, Arab states tend not to perform from the set score.

POLITICIANS AND FOREIGN SERVICE OFFICERS

Over the past half century, only a handful of politicians or top ranking government officials have adopted or advocated what might be characterized as pro-Arab stands. William Fulbright (Democratic Senator, Arkansas, 1945–74) was perhaps the best known U.S. senator who questioned the wisdom of U.S. policies in the Middle East. Although Fulbright's position was far removed from what most Palestinians demanded (he did not call for the creation of a Palestinian state) he supported additional aid to the Palestinian refugees and argued against increased arms deals and financial aid solely to Israel.[7] He adopted these positions both because he believed them to be in the best interests of the United States and because he believed there was a moral obligation to do so.

As senator, Albert Gore (D-Tenn.) served on the Foreign Relations Committee with Fulbright and was obviously influenced by his views. Gore argued that the problems in Middle East, particularly that of the Palestinians, went far beyond mere economics. In the immediate aftermath of the 1967 war, Gore stated that Israel should not make Palestinian repatriation dependent upon the signing of a peace treaty with the Arab states and that the problem had been made more complex by the displaced persons who had fled the West Bank during the 1967 war. It was not altogether coincidental that after losing his bid for reelection in the 1970s, Gore became an outspoken champion for economic assistance and close ties between Israel and the United States.

A handful of other politicians, notably Charles Percy (Republican Senator, Illinois 1967–85) and Paul Findley (Republican Senator, Illinois, 1961–83) advocated more even-handed policies. In letters and public statements to the president, vice president, secretary of state and others, they criticized U.S. policies as well as the continued Israeli attacks into Lebanon. In a 1979 letter to President Carter, Findley presciently observed that if the U.S. failed to stop Israel from using "indiscriminate violence" it would not be surprising for the Palestinians to use violence against both Israelis and Americans. He concluded that, "If that tragic time comes, the blood will be upon the hands – and the conscience – of all those who have the ability to prevent it."[8] In the light of 9/11, Findley's warnings have particular resonance. However, his criticisms of Israeli actions led to a backlash against him and he lost his bid for reelection after pro-Zionist lobby forces threw their weight (and money) behind his previously unknown opponent. He has since written several books on the strength of the Zionist lobby and the dangers to the United States posed by its unbalanced policies regarding Israel and the Palestinians.[9]

The few politicians of Arab American heritage have also publicized and pushed for Arab causes and more even handed U.S. policies; these include Senator James Abourezk (D-North Dakota), Nick Rahall (Rep. D-West Virginia), Mary Rose Oakar (Rep. D-Ohio).

Retired foreign service officers have also supported a more balanced U.S. foreign policy, while using their access in the corridors of power to educate and explain the Arab and Islamic world. For example, George Ball, often referred to as the "wise man" in U.S. diplomatic circles and who publicly opposed U.S. involvement in the Vietnam War, advised President Carter in the mid-1970s to champion the implementation of U.N. resolution 242. Ball argued that a redress of Palestinian demands and the end to the Israeli occupation of land taken in the 1967 war was in the long range interests of both Israel and US.[10]

The Middle East Institute, led by a number of retired career foreign service officers has long published a scholarly journal and held seminars and conferences aimed primarily at decision-makers "inside the beltway" (Washington insiders). But the Institute is much more low key and enjoys considerably less media coverage than pro-Zionist Washington based think tanks. Since 1981, the American Educational Trust led by retired U.S. foreign service officers Andrew I. Killgore and Richard H. Curtiss, has published the *Washington Report on the Middle East* ten times a year. The journal is widely distributed in Washington and among private subscribers. It seeks to

> provide the American public with balanced and accurate information concerning U.S. relations with Middle Eastern states ... As a solution to the Palestinian-Israeli dispute, it endorses U.N. Security Council Resolution 242's land-for-peace formula ... [and] supports Middle East solutions which it judges to be consistent with the charter of the United Nations and traditional American support for human rights, self-determination, and fair play.[11]

Every two years it also publishes a fulsome compilation of pro-Israel PAC contributions. Like most other groups on both sides of the political divide it maintains a website.

The National Council on U.S. Arab Relations led by John Duke Anthony also hosts seminars and a website. The Council sponsors Malone Fellows,[12] educational tours to Arab states for teachers, especially on the secondary and university level. In 1999 it created the *Gulf Wire Digest*, available on the Internet, to give frequent news updates and in-depth analysis on the region. After the 2003 war and the spate of anti-Saudi media campaigns, a website, Saudi-American Forum, was established to provide "information designed to provide timely information on background and current issues impacting the U.S.- Saudi relationship." It has action alerts[13] and posts information designed to improve the image of Saudi Arabia.

In addition, the Middle East Policy Council (formerly American Arab Affairs Council) established in 1981 publishes a scholarly journal, *Middle East Policy*, to "expand public discussion and understanding of issued affecting U.S. policy in the Middle East" as well as organizing workshops, conferences and contacts on Capitol Hill.

A new think tank, the Institute for Research: Middle Eastern Policy (IRMEP) was established in 2002.

> Unlike the American Enterprise Institute, Brookings Saban Center, Hudson Institute, Middle East Forum and the Washington Institute for Middle East Policy funding for IRMEP ... does not derive primarily from groups or individuals and sources promoting hidden agendas. IRMEP base support comes from ... concerned individuals who are alarmed by the current direction and authors of U.S. policies ... IRMEP also derives corporate support from U.S. industries that have faced tremendous challenges in developing their Middle East consumer and enterprise markets in the current policy environment.[14]

The institute publishes informational materials and sponsors educational conferences with a scholarly focus.

Finally, numerous institutes and academic centers deal with the Middle East. These are generally housed in major universities and attempt to provide solid and balanced research and programs on the region. These centers and scholars are not spokespeople for the government policies of any regime in Middle East, but seek to provide scholarly, well-researched and documented material that may variously be favorable or critical of all regimes, including Israel.

After the 11 September attacks, some Israeli supporters sought to take advantage of the prevalent atmosphere of hysteria by launching slur campaigns against the academic integrity of these centers and specific academics. Daniel Pipes, founder of the pro-Israeli Middle East Institute in Washington, heads the so-called Campus Watch that names U.S. academics whose work – however scholarly and well-researched – can be construed in any way as critical of Israel. Attempts to silence the voices of scholars whose views contradict the policies of the neo-conservatives in Washington or the Zionist lobby culminated in moves to undercut and oversee government funding through Title VI of the National Defense Education Act of 1958 and the Higher Education Act of 1965. Title VI grants supply financial support for graduate studies, language training and community outreach programs for over 100 centers focused on regional area studies such as Asia, Latin America, the Middle East and Africa. Although only 17 centers for Middle East studies in U.S. universities receive Title VI funding, these programs were singled out for Congressional and media criticism. By 2003/04, new legislation (HR 3077) to create an independent seven-member advisory board for Title VI programs had been unanimously approved in the House was making its way through the Senate. The board would include members from national security agencies (Department of Defense/CIA) and was charged with monitoring and evaluating the Title VI programs. Scholars, university centers and notably Senator Ted Kennedy spoke out vigorously against the possibility of a return to 1950s McCarthyism with its witch-hunts against alleged Communists. The prospective witch-hunts of the twenty-first century would be against those who, based on long term and intimate knowledge of the region, have correctly pointed out the fallacies and failures of U.S. foreign policy in Iran, Afghanistan, Iraq and Israel.

HUMAN RIGHTS ORGANIZATIONS

Although some human rights organizations dealing with the Middle East focus on civil liberties and the status of women and children, many center on Palestine, in particular the plight of the Palestinians. Church and community activist groups tend to dominate these organizations that include, among others, the Palestine Aid Society, United Holy Land Fund, the Quaker, American Friends Service Committee (AFSC) and the highly effective Palestine Human Rights Campaign (PHRC). PHRC was established in 1977 to "1. Promote the investigation, publication and understanding of these incidents of human rights violations, 2. lend support to the victims and their attornies [sic], 3. secure enforcement of existing internationally recognized norms of human rights and fundamental freedoms for the Palestinian people."[15] From 1980 to 1989 Rev. Donald E. Wagner served as PHRC national director. James Zoghby, based in Washington, worked with the PHRC in the 1970s. The group issued bulletins, held conferences and public demonstrations, and mobilized church and human rights activists around the single issue of Palestinian rights. PHRC successfully rallied a segment of the U.S. public around human rights; its campaigns resonated with the public far more effectively than attempts by the Arab League or Arab governments that had at their disposal far greater funds and resources.

Donald Wagner became an expert on Christian involvement, particularly by evangelicals, in the Middle East. He went on to lead Evangelicals for Middle East Understanding (established in 1986) for a decade. Along similar lines, Sabeel (meaning "the way" or "channel") was founded by ten church and laypersons in 1989 as an ecumenical grassroots organization. Sabeel maintains a website, publishes a newsletter and sponsors trips and conferences. Without massive economic support, it raises funds by selling Christmas cards and other items; Sabeel emphasizes the rights of Palestinians, particularly Christian Palestinians, and the status of Jerusalem.

The membership of these human rights groups often overlaps and many of the same professionals have been involved in several or more of these organizations. All struggle to stay afloat financially; all are underfunded and lack endowments. They survive by small contributions and the efforts of committed volunteers. Their efforts are directed primarily toward mobilizing public/citizen support for the cause of human rights – especially for the Palestinians – and are not primarily focused on influencing Washington.

PETROLEUM INDUSTRY AND BUSINESS INTERESTS

Private businesses with interests in the Arab world, particularly the petroleum industry, also try to influence policies regarding the Middle East. They tend to rely on personal contacts and friendships with policy-makers and prefer to work quietly behind the scenes. They rarely attempt to mobilize public opinion or to launch major media campaigns on specific issues. Although the public believes that the petroleum industry has had major impacts on U.S. policy in the Middle East, the reality is that the industry's influence has been far greater in securing favorable domestic legislation than on matters pertaining to the Middle East. To placate oil producing Arab nations, the industry has quietly argued for a more balanced approach to the Arab Israeli conflict, but it has had virtually no success in this regard. On the other hand, U.S. officials worked hard to maintain favorable relations with regimes in oil-producing nations, in particular Saudi Arabia. They did so, not so much because of pressure from the oil industry, but owing to the perceived wisdom that the free flow of oil at the lowest possible prices were in the best interests of the United States.[16]

The importance of Saudi Arabia to U.S. strategic and economic interests has historically been a stumbling block in the Zionist lobby's hostility to all Arab states. Stuart Eizenstat, a staunch Zionist in the Carter White House, described the problem of vilifying OPEC while allaying Saudi concerns.

Now there are other instances, Saudi Arabia being a perfect example which has been a good friend of this administration's and of this country's, it's kept its production higher in its own economic and national interests, it's done so to keep some stability in the world markets, and Lord knows where we would be if we didn't have that. There are other countries like Libya, Iraq and others, who have not been as modern and as sensible.[17]

Eizenstat's remarks highlight a curious, but all too common, tendency to ascribe "positive" qualities to those Arab regimes that adopt pro-U.S. policies, while denigrating and actively confronting those who take opposing or neutral positions.

Under this rubric, Saudi Arabia, one of the most traditional if not reactionary states in the region, can be described as "modern" while Iraq, a dictatorship, but with a far more progressive social, cultural, and economic system is deemed less "modern." By any objective, scholarly criteria, Iraq, particularly in the 1970s and 1980s, was undoubtedly far more "modern" and secular than Saudi Arabia. Similarly, when Arab leaders, even dictators such as Sadat, adopt pro-U.S. policies they are immediately labeled as "moderate."

With the first Gulf War, the U.S. increasingly dropped the pretense of pacifying so-called "moderate," or "modern" regimes in favor of direct military intervention to assure the free flow of oil at low prices. The Zionist lobby gave its fulsome, whole hearted support for this more direct approach that served to guarantee Israeli and U.S. hegemony over the entire Middle East.

By the 1990s, Arab American business people had also entered the stage. A spate of new journals and organizations such as the Arab American Chamber of Commerce appeared. The Chamber was active in launching joint conferences with Arab governments/investors, Arab Americans and private corporations. Magazines such as *Arab American Business* publicized itself as "The Magazine for a Culture of Success;" while the *Arab American Almanac* provided an extensive directory of Arab American organizations and leaders nationwide. These groups have yet to see their political stances regarding the Arab world influence either political life in the U.S. or foreign policy.

ETHNIC ORGANIZATIONS

Finally, Arab Americans like other ethnic groups such as the Poles, Irish and Greeks, have mobilized, with varying degrees of success, around specific issues. Because Arab Americans are not specifically classified in the U.S. census exact statistics on the numbers of Arab Americans are difficult to obtain. Experts agree that there is an undercount of Arab Americans in the U.S. census.[18] There are two main reasons for the undercount: first, census forms do not have a separate category for Arabs so individuals must self select to write in "Arab" as their ethnic affiliation, and second, built in cultural fears about possible government reprisals result in avoidance or refusal to participate in the census. In the 2000 census there were an estimated 1.2 million Arab Americans, an increase from the 610,000 estimated in the 1980 census.[19] By the 2000s, the Census Bureau estimated there were 1.5 million Arab Americans, although Arab American organizations put the numbers as high as 3.5 million, or slightly over 1 percent of the U.S. population. About half of all Arab Americans live in six mainly northern, industrial states (Illinois, Massachusetts, Ohio, Pennsylvania, and Texas) with the single highest concentration in Michigan where they could constitute over 5 percent of overall votes in a presidential election. Clustered in these key urban states as well as California, Arab Americans thereby have the potential for far greater political clout. Interestingly most Jewish Americans are also clustered in the key states of Pennsylvania, Ohio, Florida, Michigan, and California. An estimated 78 percent of the Muslim vote went to the Republican George W. Bush in the 2000 presidential election; however, in the 2004 election both the Arab American and Muslim vote was essentially "up for grabs."[20]

As crises and wars continue throughout much of the Arab world, people continue to immigrate to the United States and the Arab American population continues to grow. However, The Patriot Acts and other erosions of civil rights and liberties following the 11 September 2001 attacks will result in a decline of the number of Arab immigrants over the short term and will also exacerbate the problems of convincing an already fearful and insecure Arab American population to proclaim its ethnic affiliation in the census or to become involved politically.

Although their population figures are similar to the numbers of Greek Americans, Arab Americans have never had a lobbying success on the level enjoyed by Greek Americans over the Cyprus crisis and their victories in instituting and maintaining an arms embargo on Turkey. Obviously, no other ethic group has ever achieved anything close to the power of Jewish American lobby groups in influencing and fashioning U.S. foreign policy.

Among Arab Americans, churches and clubs representing particular villages or areas date back to the nineteenth century. More politically-focused organizations only emerged during the 1960s and 1970s. The disastrous defeat of the Arabs in the 1967 war impelled some Arab Americans to establish organizations to combat prevailing anti-Arab prejudices and to pressure Washington to adopt policies more favorable to the Arab world.

The 1970s were heady times when a number of differing trends emerged among the older Arab American communities and the newer immigrant communities. By the 1990s some 70 Arab American organizations had headquarters or chapters in Washington, D.C.,[21] but only a handful enjoyed national recognition.

Aiming to fill the information gap about the Arab world in the U.S. a group of mainly academics formed the Association of Arab American University Graduates (AAUG) soon after the 1967 war.[22] The AAUG became a major source of information about the Arab world, publishing position papers, books and analyses, and holding annual conventions, lecture series and educational trips to the Middle East. In 1970, the AAUG created the *Arab Studies Quarterly* that remains one of the foremost scholarly journals on the region. The National Association of Arab-Americans (NAAA) was established 1972; it lobbies the U.S. Congress and writes to the White House and Congress on specific issues of import to Arab Americans and the Middle East. The American-Arab Anti-Discrimination Committee (ADC), led by former Democratic Senator from North Dakota James AbouRezk, was established in 1980. Under his dynamic, charismatic leadership, ADC quickly became the foremost advocate for Arab Americans. The late Dr. Hala Maksoud was a highly visible and effective leader of ADC during the 1990s. In 2003 former Democratic congresswoman from Ohio Mary Rose Oakar became ADC President. ADC has been most successful in domestic issues pertaining to ethnic intimidation, stereotypes and court cases. It hosts a summer intern program for young Arab Americans and others as well as underwriting a think tank, the ADC Research Institute (ADCRI), to "train a pro-active, experienced generation of future leaders."

Arab American organizations have not only faced political opposition from the opposing Zionist lobby but have also been the targets of violent attacks. There have been innumerable threats against Arab American leaders as well as hate mail, emails attacks and harassment. The Washington PHRC office was fire-bombed in 1980 and ADC offices have also been attacked. These culminated in the killing of ADC West Coast Director Alex Odeh in a bomb attack in 1985. The FBI launched a protracted investigation of this attack and suspected members of the Jewish Defense League (JDL) of involvement, but to date there have been no convictions for his murder.[23]

James Zogby, who had been involved in the leadership of a number of Arab American organizations, established the Arab American Institute (AAI) in 1985. Zogby and the AAI encourage Arab American participation in politics on local and national levels. AAI works to mobilize Arab Americans to vote as well as to run for office. Zogby and other Arab American activists have been heartened by the involvement of the new generation of Arab Americans who were born in the U.S. and who do not feel inhibited by foreign accents or feelings of inferiority regarding their "Americanness." As they say, "We must tell our own stories."[24] This new generation will undoubtedly become more visible and influential. American Muslims have also become increasingly active and have established a number of organizations including the Council on American Islamic Relations (CAIR) with 13 offices around the nation and the Muslim Public Affairs Council (MPAC) based in Los Angeles.

However, these groups are all relatively small and under-financed. They have often been plagued by the same divisiveness that separates the Arab nations and often fail to mount unified effective programs. Historically most have been patriarchal and personality driven. The AAUG was noticeably different in this regard: from its inception it held open elections and women served on the board and as president. Finally, with very few exceptions, Arab Americans still do not hold many high ranking positions within the government.

ARAB AMERICANS AND WASHINGTON

Before lobbyists can effectively push for changes in U.S. foreign policy, they must gain access to government officials. Having done so they must then counter the built in cultural hostility toward Arabs and Muslims. As a result, Arab Americans often expend considerable time and effort proclaiming their "Americanness" and their loyalty to the U.S. government. Events following 9/11 exacerbated this trend.

Although the White House communicates with ethnic groups through liaisons or offices of ethnic affairs based in the White House, contacts or meetings with Arab Americans are treated as matters of foreign, not domestic policy. They must be approved or rejected by the State Department or NSC. The treatment accorded to NAAA, one of the leading Arab American organizations during President Ford's most publicized "reassessment" of Middle East policy, is indicative of the relationship between Arab Americans and presidents. After the NSC labeled as "inadvisable" repeated requests for a meeting with the president, NAAA responded by adopting a carrot and stick technique. NAAA included complimentary remarks about the Ford presidency in its newsletter, but followed up by bringing the White House rejection to the attention of the press in letters to the editor of both the *New York Times* and the *Washington Post*, with copies sent to the White House. Although Henry Kissinger continued to oppose the meeting, others in the NSC countered that the meeting should take place because Kissinger could control the substance and nature of any meeting with the NAAA. Records of the subsequent meeting indicate that Kissinger did, in fact, dominate the conversation. President Ford had pre-prepared talking points (prior to meetings, presidents receive lists of prepared answers for possible topics of conversation) on the Lebanon crisis, U.S. aid to Israel and the Palestinians. But these issues were not raised! Thus Ford and Kissinger easily avoided having to confront the major and potentially volatile issues regarding U.S. policy. For the press, the White House could honestly affirm that the meeting was part of Ford's attempt to "solicit views" and that it had had no impact on policy decisions.[25]

Subsequent presidents have been no more eager to meet with Arab Americans. Under Carter, individual Arab Americans, the AAUG, NAAA and American Lebanese League all pressed for a direct meeting with the president. In efforts to assuage mounting pressure, a meeting with NAAA and Midge Costanza, Carter's public liaison, was arranged in February 1977. Costanza's office had a long list of ethnic groups with whom she was to communicate. Groups from the Middle East were divided into a number of categories, some of which were incomprehensible or even bizarre; groups deemed major were also underlined. The list included: Arabs, Armenians, Egyptians, Iraqis, Israelis, Jordanians, Lebanese and "S. Arabian"s. Although there are a number of Americans of Palestinian descent, they were not included. Armenians, "S. Arabians" and Lebanese were underlined. "S. Arabians" may have stood for Saudi Arabians, even though scarcely any U.S. citizens are of Saudi descent, or, perhaps Yemenis (Southern Arabian). European ethnic groups such as Italians, Lithuanians, Romanians, Russians, Serbians, Slovenians, Ukrainians were all underlined.[26] Jewish Americans were not on the list as they have their own separate liaison. At the February meeting with Costanza, members of the

NAAA discussed a range of domestic issues but matters of foreign policy, particularly the Arab Israeli conflict and the inclusion of the Palestinians in Carter's peace process, were not raised.

In November, several members from the AAUG met with Secretary of State Cyrus Vance and presented a statement calling for the inclusion of the PLO in the peace process along with the recognition of Palestinian rights.[27] However, as the peace process proceeded, Arab American organizations continued to request a meeting with the president.

But it took pressure from Arab American Congresspersons Rahall and Oakar (both Democrats) and other high-ranking officials, as well as protracted letter writing campaigns, before Arab Americans finally met with Carter late in 1977. When the Arab American organizations were initially put off with excuses that the president was too busy to meet with them, they retorted that although they had supported the president, Jewish Americans had been granted meetings while their requests had been denied.[28]

NSC adviser Zbigniew Brzezinski was particularly reluctant to meet with the Arab Americans or to agree to a meeting with Carter. Brzezinski only agreed to a meeting with Arab Americans after repeated pressure, particularly from NSC staff advisers William Quandt and Gary Sick. Quandt and Sick argued that:

> … it is safe to assume that we will be hearing from this group more frequently (and effectively) in the future than in the past.
>
> The advantages of a brief meeting are not great. It would avoid giving offense to a small but increasingly vocal group and would be received with satisfaction by the Arab-American community and the Arab states of the Middle East. Likewise, the disadvantages are not particularly worrisome. Although it would not be welcomed by Israel's supporters, it could hardly be viewed as a one-sided gesture. At worst, it might be viewed as a mild rebuke in the wake of the settlements controversy.[29]

In a hand-written note, Brzezinski retorted, "talk to me, I am very skeptical."[30] After reviewing a large number of letters from Arab Americans, Brzezinski then told Hamilton Jordan that "On foreign policy grounds, I do not recommend that the President meet with this group."[31] However, after the Arab American organizations and Quandt kept up the pressure, Brzezinski relented.

In his subsequent memo to Carter, Bzrezinski repeated almost verbatim Quandt's arguments for meeting with Arab Americans, telling the president that he intended to meet with a small group of Arab American leaders for 45 minutes and asking if Carter could stop by the meeting for 10–15 minutes.[32]

Finally, six months after Jewish Americans had met with the White House and following months of pressure, Arab Americans met with Carter on 15 December 1977.[33] The meeting was another well-orchestrated White House event. The White House purposely avoided having to deal with only one issue – namely the Palestinian demands for statehood – by inviting a diverse group of Arab Americans, personally adding the American Lebanese League to the list of invitees. As with the Ford administration, the Carter White House, particularly the NSC, wanted to defuse pressure or criticism by including as broad a spectrum of groups as possible.

First, 15 Arab American leaders met with Assistant Secretary State Warren Christopher. They were joined by Bzrezinski who sat "glumly" in a seating arrangement that placed Carter between advisers, not Arab Americans. When Carter joined the meeting, Brzezinski left. At the time, the Arab Americans were unaware that earlier on the same day Carter had announced in a nation wide press conference that the PLO was not a "serious consideration" in the peace talks.

A member of the American Lebanese League spoke first and was the only one to present a statement that included a rather long and time consuming exposition about their loyalty and pride in being American. Carter then spoke at length about his involvement in the peace process and his attempts to talk with the Palestinians. He noted that he had taken a lot of political heat for his efforts and that the PLO had not lived up to their agreements. AAUG President Michael Suleiman explained that the PLO rejected U.N. Resolution 242 because it did not specifically mention the Palestinians.

Carter quickly retorted that he did not care if the PLO had 30 pages of reservations as long as it accepted the resolution. As the meeting ended, AAUG, NAAA and the Ramallah Association attempted to present Carter with statements that urged the PLO be included in the negotiations. AAUG member Fouad Moughrabi, of Palestinian descent, also tried to give the president the key to his parent's home in Palestine, but Carter refused both the statements and the key.

When a protracted search by this author and helpful archivists at the Carter Presidential Library failed to locate the reports, minutes, or follow ups from this meeting, the archivists hazarded a guess that some NSC officials might have taken them.[34] Thus, although the meeting involved Americans, not foreign officials, it was treated as a matter of foreign policy and defense concern, not as a domestic matter or for the public liaison.[35] Similarly, in contrast to letters or meetings with other American domestic pressure groups, correspondence and meetings with Arab Americans and Arab American organizations are not in the public liaison files, but in National Defense (NSC) files and are dealt with by that office.

To put the meeting in perspective regarding its importance in Carter's schedule; his daily diary for 15 December notes that the meeting with Arab Americans took 30 minutes, a meeting with representatives from church related colleges, five minutes, and the lighting of the Christmas tree, 32 minutes.[36]

The Clinton administration's meeting with leaders from Arab American organizations in the White House during the first 100 days in office is a recognition of the increased participation and impact of Arab American organizations. However, their involvement on the domestic front has not necessarily translated into impact on foreign policy.

FINANCES

Although Arab American activists complain about the difficulties in mobilizing the community, organizational problems and lack of unity, finances remain one of the biggest obstacles to their effective lobby efforts. Arab Americans have a higher than average income but give less. The major Arab American organizations all lack substantial endowments and most operate on an almost day-to-day basis. The failure to develop a sound financial foundation for political efforts means that activists must spend considerable time and effort not on lobby campaigns, but on raising money to make any efforts possible.

A comparison of Arab American/Muslim PACs with pro-Israeli PACs demonstrates the disparity. In 1984, pro-Arab PACs raised $17,350 in contrast to pro-Israeli PACs that raised $3,772,994, or a ratio of 147–1; by 1996 the figures had improved only marginally from $20,625 to $2,738,647 or a ratio of 133–1.[37] Without major financial support, no protracted lobby effort or media campaign is possible.

In the last decade a much wider spectrum of Arab Americans have entered the political arena and they have gained greater access to the White House and other government offices, but this has yet to be translated into greater effectiveness in altering U.S. foreign policy.[38] Then, too, just as they were becoming more active and involved, their programs and activities were impeded by the Patriot Act and other restrictions on the everyday life of Arab Americans that were enacted following the 11 September attacks.

Still, activists seek to emphasize the mutual goals of Arab Americans and the general U.S. public. In 1993, Zogby emphasized, during a conference that attracted eight of the nine Democratic presidential hopefuls (Joseph Lieberman, a Jewish American with a well-known pro-Israeli stance, perhaps understandably chose not to attend), that "Our issues are your issues."[39] AAI issued a 2004 voter guide on Democratic Presidential Candidates[40] that detailed their stands on Israel and Palestine, Immigration, Civil Liberties and U.S. Arab Relations.

In an indication of their growing presence, an Arab American activist, Imad Hamad, based in Dearborn, Michigan, was to receive the FBI's Exceptional Public Service Award in 2003 for his assistance in the aftermath of 9/11. However, after a minor columnist, Debbie Schlussel, and the Zionist Organization of America (ZOA) launched a vindictive campaign against giving any Arab American such an award, the FBI withdrew the nomination. Although the media in Michigan, with a large, informed and active Arab American community covered the slur campaign against Hamad, the incident attracted little national attention.[41] The racial aspects of the Zionist attacks against an entire ethnic group went unnoticed by the general public that, as described earlier, have become largely inured to racist treatment of Arabs and Muslims.

Thus, in the face of steady pressure by pro-Israeli groups, the Christian right, now in the ascendancy in Washington, and the general public's hostility to Arabs and Muslims, most politicians remain reluctant to deal openly with Arabs, even those who are "courted" by the United States.

7
The Cast: Jewish Americans and Pro-Zionist Lobbies

The Zionist lobby is a multi-armed force that includes the state of Israel, Jewish American groups, their allies in government and other pro-Zionist interest groups. Israel and the Zionist lobby often act as an anti-Arab and anti-Muslim lobby. Zionists in the U.S. advocate unquestioned financial support for Israel, U.S. backing for Israel in international organizations, particularly the United Nations, pro-Israel policies regarding the Middle East and anti-Arab policies. The Zionist lobby works assiduously to limit or obstruct open, objective debate on the Arab Israeli conflict, Middle East history and discussion of Palestinian rights to self-determination.

ISRAEL

From its inception, Israel recognized the importance of lobbies and interest groups and devoted considerable resources and effort to study how they work within the U.S. system.[1] Unlike the Arab states, from 1948 onward, Israel has supported institutes such as the Jaffee Center, devoted to the study of the U.S. political system. Israeli academic experts routinely advise Israeli prime ministers, while centers for strategic studies based in Israeli universities keep the Israeli government informed on the ebb and flow of domestic policies in the U.S. as well as on matters pertaining to the Middle East.

The Israeli embassy in Washington and consulates around the U.S. frequently mount information campaigns by providing speakers and Israeli students to attend conferences, and participate in community events. Israel has long recognized the importance of "hasbara," or information for the non-Jewish world. Consequently, Israeli embassies regularly host lunches and meetings for teachers, community activists, students and politicians as well as sponsoring trips to Israel for journalists, church leaders and others. Embassies send lists of resources on publications, policy papers on issues of relevance to Israel, as well as providing background papers, to a wide range of Jewish Americans, academics, teachers and community organizations. In addition, they also keep track and often attend academic conferences dealing with all aspects of the Middle East.[2]

In contrast to Arab governments, Israel frequently coordinates single, unified lobby efforts with U.S. based groups, thereby avoiding overlap of effort and strengthening the overall effectiveness of their programs.[3] Familiarity with the U.S. system enables the Israeli embassy to manipulate U.S. political realities to its own advantage.

JEWISH AMERICAN ORGANIZATIONS

The impact of Jewish American lobbying efforts far exceeds the demographic presence of the community in the United States. In 2000, there were an estimated 5.2 million Jewish Americans, a 5 percent decline from the 1990s.[4] This is between 2.2 percent and 2.5 percent of U.S. population. These communities are concentrated in five main states. Interestingly, these estimates closely parallel those of Arab Americans. However, unlike Arab Americans, the numbers of Jewish Americans continues to fall owing largely to a 52 percent intermarriage rate. Orthodox Jews, who are least likely to marry outside the faith, are only 9.7 percent of American Jews; conservatives are 15.2 percent and 17.4 percent as classified as reform, with an almost 60–70 percent intermarriage rate.[5]

Only a small percentage of Jewish Americans are active in the Zionist movement. Perhaps only a third or less of Jewish Americans give financial support to the Zionist project.[6] In the 1990s fully 78 percent thought Israel should freeze Jewish settlements and 79 percent supported a demilitarized Palestinian state.[7] The majority of American Jews, although emotionally sympathetic to Israel as a Jewish state, do not share a hard-line Likud party approach to questions involving Palestinians, a two state solution, or keeping the Occupied Territories. Two thirds of Jewish Americans report that they are emotionally attached to Israel, but only 35 percent have visited the country.[8] Yet since the 1990s the major Zionist lobby groups have not reflected those attitudes. Because Jewish Americans are extremely reluctant to criticize Israel in public or to air divisions within their community before the larger American society, the hard-line stance has prevailed.

In addition, perhaps as many as 1 million Israelis currently live, more or less permanently, in the United States. An uncertain number of this little studied population has dual citizenship with full voting rights in both nations. Many are professionals and academics who take active roles in defending Israeli causes.

Jewish Americans have joined and established a multitude of organizations for religious and social welfare programs as well as in support of Zionism and the state of Israel. The American Zionist Emergency Council (AZEC) active in 1940s later evolved into the American Zionist Council. In the post World War II era, the Zionist Organization of America (ZOA), was led by Rabbi Abba Hillel Silver, a tireless campaigner for Israel. Rabbi Silver met with President Eisenhower and was in regular contact with Secretary of State John Foster Dulles.

Other major Jewish American organizations are: the Conference of American Rabbis, Hadassah, the women's Zionist organization that has a wide range of activities including promoting trips to Israel for Jewish Americans; the American Jewish Congress, with a leftist political slant and the American Jewish Committee, with a more right of center political position. It publishes *Commentary*, the main journal of opinion for many Jewish Americans. The Anti-Defamation League (ADL) and American Israel Public Affairs Committee (AIPAC) are two of the most visible Jewish American organizations in lobbying efforts. The Conference of Presidents of major American Jewish Organizations with leaders from over 30 organizations is a key umbrella organization for these various groups. By 2003 major Jewish organizations coordinated 52 national Jewish organizations. Leaders from these groups, including religious organizations, women's clubs and political action groups meet regularly to formulate long-term policies and strategies.

During the 1950s, the American Zionist Council of Public Affairs, along with other Jewish American organizations, worked to counteract perceived anti-Israeli forces in the Eisenhower administration. They constituted a chorus producing a steady stream of pro-Israeli letters, telegrams and communications. The barrage was so great that State Department officials jested that the person at the Palestine Desk had to be very tall because a short man would be "submerged by Zionist telegrams in moments of stress."[9]

A wide variety of think tanks, including the American Enterprise Institute (AEI), the Middle East Media Research Institute (Memri), the Hudson Institute, and the Washington Institute for Near East Policy (WINEP) also publicize and push for an Israeli U.S. alliance. AEI has published assets over $35 million, with an annual income of over $24 million; in contrast, the pro-Arab *Washington Report* must constantly solicit funds to continue publishing.[10] This substantial financial backing enables these centers to underwrite a wide range of programs and support for publications that far exceeds anything undertaken by pro-Arab groups. A fairly close network of analysts work in one or more of these think tanks and they tend to share a common antipathy to leftists, Arabs, Muslims, or anyone who contradicts pro-Israeli viewpoints.

Since its inception in 1985, the Washington Institute for Near East Policy (WINEP) has gained a high profile on Capitol Hill,[11] publishing policy papers, holding seminars, organizing trips to the Middle East, furnishing background information for journalists and government officials, as well as testifying before Congress. In 2002 WINEP boasted that it had placed 90 articles or op-ed pieces in leading journals over the last year. This is an astoundingly high number and is indicative of its clout in the mainstream media.

Several WINEP associates are former government officials and others have been hired for high-level government jobs. Their contacts in Israel help these think tanks to secure consulting jobs in key government agencies for their personnel,[12] thereby creating a revolving door for individuals to serve in government, then as fellows in a high level (and usually well funded) think tank and then back to government again.

However, The American Israel Public Affairs Committee (AIPAC), a registered lobby based in Washington, is arguably the most successful of all these organizations. AIPAC evolved out of American Zionist Council and was founded in 1954 by I.L. "Sy" Kenen.[13] Kenen's interpretation of AIPAC's role was "to tell the president to overrule the State Department."[14]

AIPAC operates as a clearing house and coordinator for Jewish Organizations to push a pro-Israeli agenda in the White House and Congress. AIPAC's mission is to "insure close and consistently strong U.S.–Israel relations." Leaders from a variety of Jewish organizations serve on the AIPAC board. By 1985, AIPAC had a staff of 75 with an annual budget of $5.7 million.[15] Although AIPAC claims only 50,000 members who pay $50 dues per year, it has a $15 million budget, 150 employees and half a dozen full time registered lobbyists. Among its many activities, it holds frequent policy conferences in Washington, D.C., breakfast meetings with select Jewish leaders and workshops on how to monitor and influence media. AIPAC lobbies in Washington throughout the year, and its leaders visit regularly their representatives and the staffs of key committees. It closely follows the voting records and statements of candidates and gives briefings, along with "meet with the candidates" opportunities. AIPAC caucus groups of 15–30 members, organized by congressional districts, routinely lobby members of Congress on issues pertaining to Israel. In addition, AIPAC provides campaign updates to influence political party organizations, identifying candidates with "good" or "bad" records of support for Israel. It then works to defeat those with so-called "bad records" as, for example, Charles Percy and Paul Findley. AIPAC also publishes the weekly *Near East Report* and issues "Action Alerts" on government actions that affect Israel in negative ways.

In recognition of the potential of information campaigns for changing minds and influencing foreign policy, AIPAC issues a constant stream of publications and policy papers presenting Israel as a loyal and valuable ally for the United States and often portraying the Arabs in negative terms. AIPAC regularly sends *Facts and Myths* and *Near East Report* to hundreds of White House officials, members of Congress and their aides, and other government officials. By 1990s *Near East Report* claimed a circulation of over 40,000.

Although these publications purport to provide balanced and factual coverage, they are, in fact, consistently pro-Israeli and anti-Arab. In 1974 AIPAC joined forces with a number of other Jewish organizations to counter any "pro-Arab" voices. As editor of *Near East Report*, Kenen tracked individuals or groups that took pro-Arab stances, who criticized Israel, or who expressed opposition to the pro-Israeli policies adopted in Washington. A network of zealous university students and supporters expand upon these activities by depicting Israel in the most favorable light and Arabs in the most negative terms throughout the nation. Their efforts reinforce the prevalent stereotypic depiction of Arabs/Muslims in the media and popular culture.

In 1974, Morris Amitay succeeded Kenen as Executive Director of AIPAC. Amitay made AIPAC into a major lobby force in Washington. Thomas Dine and Steven Grossman took over as directors in the 1980s and 1990s respectively. By the 1990s, AIPAC was considered the second most effective lobby in the country, ranking only behind AARP (American Association of Retired Persons, with 33 million members). AIPAC thereby exceeded the power and clout of even organized labor. Members of Congress are keenly aware of AIPAC's political and financial power and pay close attention to its activities. In recognition of AIPAC's influence, over half the members of Congress attended at least one event during AIPAC's 2004 annual conference.

In the 1980s, Dine expanded AIPAC's activities to encompass anti-Arab programs. A full time employee from ADL was hired to track opponents or so-called "enemies" of Israel. Although when it was originally established in 1913 the ADL was the foremost watch dog in the valuable work of defending Jews and other minorities against anti-Semitism, racism and hate crimes, by the early 1960s it increasingly equated any anti-Zionist or anti-Israeli stance with anti-Semitism and included peace groups and leftists in its list of potential enemies. Consequently, ADL "blacklisted" and infiltrated over two dozen peace organizations as well as Arab American groups, including organizations or individuals that criticized Israel or supported human rights for Palestinians. ADL went so far as to videotape funerals of Palestinians in the mid-West.[16] This information on U.S. citizens was then passed on to the FBI and the Israeli government. ADL's circulation of the names of academics and campus activists who spoke out against Israeli abuses, prompted the Middle East Studies Association (MESA), some of whose members had attracted the wrath of AIPAC and earned places on the "enemies list," to condemn both the AIPAC and ADL blacklisting in 1984.

In 1993, ADC, AAUG, the Committee in Solidarity With the People of El Salvador, the International Jewish Peace Union, the National Conference of Black Lawyers, and others filed a class action suit against the ADL.[17] The case slowly wended its way through the legal labyrinth and resulted in a permanent injunction against the ADL for spying on Arab Americans. But AIPAC's "Policy Analysis" section continued under Michael Lewis (son of Bernard Lewis, considered by some as the current resident intellectual on the Middle East and Islamic world for George W. Bush), to monitor so-called enemies of Israel. In a Weekly Activities publication the names of groups and people critical of Israel are sent to select Jewish leaders, citizens and the Israeli Embassy. After the 11 September attacks, criticism of so-called Arabists escalated. Websites and public critiques appeared condemning specific academics who had, in most cases, merely stated facts about the political and historic realities of the Arab and Muslim world that the Zionists and neo-conservatives did not wish to hear. The Zionist success as an anti-Arab and anti-Muslim force is a major stumbling block to more objective analysis of the Middle East.

AIPAC also boasts of its success in assuring that Congress remains pro-Israel and has bragged about defeating Charles Percy who had incurred its wrath by criticizing Israel.[18] George McGovern observed that not giving Israel what it wanted in arms/aid/support was "a great political risk" because within an hour calls would come flooding in from Washington and states/districts.[19] A senior State Department official, speaking on condition of anonymity, added that AIPAC "tends to skew the consideration of issues ... people don't look very hard at some options."[20] With its proven ability to deliver votes and channel money to candidates and punish its enemies, AIPAC is a "star" performer in Washington.

Using this power, AIPAC and pro-Israeli think tanks regularly arrange meetings between government officials and select Middle East "experts." Under the presidency of George W. Bush, these groups have formed an alliance with both the Christian right and the neo-conservatives and have what is commonly considered the inside track in the White House. In words of Hamilton Jordan, AIPAC's "collective mobilizing ability is unsurpassed in terms of the quality and quantity of political communications that can be triggered on specific issues perceived to be critical of Israel."[21]

PRO-ISRAELI LOBBIES AND U.S. GOVERNMENT

For over 50 years, stalwart pro-Israeli representatives and senators have championed the Israeli cause. In the Senate and House, with a total of 535 members, over half are firm or very sympathetic supporters of Israel. Less than a handful (three to six) could be deemed to be sympathetic to the Arabs.[22] As many politicians are reelected time and again they become chairs of key Congressional committees and wield considerable power. Support for Israel cuts across party lines, geographic regions and religious or ethnic affiliations. Jewish American politicians, many with long tenures in the House and Senate, are forceful advocates for the Zionist cause. These included, during the 1960s and 1970s, Emanuel Celler (D-NY), who was elected to 25 succeeding Congresses; Lester Wolff (D-NY), Abraham Ribicoff (D-CT), Benjamin Rosenthal (D-NY) and in the Senate, Jacob Javits (R-NY). On the other hand, some politicians from states with very small Jewish populations, notably Henry "Scoop" Jackson (D-Washington State) have been flamboyant spokespersons for Israel. Jackson mentored a number of young ambitious staff members, mostly notably Richard Perle, who went on to become a well-known and exceedingly vocal champion of neo-conservative and Israeli causes.

Moving easily from America to Israel, Jewish Americans also act as cultural go-betweens. Some like Richard Perle are neo-conservatives as well as Zionists and, in fact, equate the two ideologies, blending the two for mutual gain. Others may be committed to the Israeli cause but hold a variety of political outlooks.

The career of Stuart Eizenstat is typical. An attorney from Atlanta, Georgia, Eizenstat was an early Carter supporter; observers noted that Eizenstat had been "bitten by the political bug." Through hard work and keen intellect, he developed an impressive resume: serving as Assistant to the President for Domestic Affairs and Policy under Carter, and during the Clinton administration holding several top level positions including Deputy Treasury Secretary, Under Secretary of State for Economic, Business and Agricultural Affairs and Under Secretary of Commerce for International Trade.[23] He was Ambassador to the European Union from 1993 to 1996, served on the board of advisers for WINEP (pro-Israeli Washington Institute for Near East Policy) and provided Clinton with position papers on the Middle East.

In some regards, Eizenstat might be characterized as a liberal democrat; for example, he supported the Kyoto accord to limit global warming,[24] but he has also expressed his admiration for Henry Kissinger's foreign policy strategies. A self-described "head hunter" to identify and recommend personnel for the Carter administration,[25] Eizenstat has been forthright about his commitment to Israel, consistently advocating pro-Israeli policies and recommending people that favored Israel for key government jobs. Although he was involved with domestic issues in the Carter White House, Eizenstat persistently requested that he receive wire traffic from Israel and that he be included in foreign policy meetings. Senior Adviser and conduit to the Jewish American community Edward Sanders was equally tenacious in his requests to be included in "the working sessions of the American delegation at Camp David" as well as asking to travel with the president to Camp David.[26] The NSC and State Department sought to deflect these requests as far as possible, but they indicate a keen awareness by champions of the Israeli cause of the importance of having a presence and – if possible – a voice in top level meetings involving policy decisions.

But Eizenstat's commitment to Israel went further than mere interest in U.S. Israeli relations. In a speech at the California think tank, the Susan and David Wilstein Institute of Jewish Policy Studies in Los Angeles in 1989, Eizenstat bluntly summarized his views on what some might well consider a problem of dual loyalty.

No longer was Middle East policy the sole province of largely Arabist scholars. Serious thinkers like Martin Indyk of the Washington Institute for Near East Policy and Steven Spiegel of UCLA gained prominence ... In the Bush Administration, we see the flowering of Jewish scholars entering positions of influence in the State Department and National Security Council involving Middle East policy. They feel no conflict between their Jewish identification and their sympathetic attitude toward Israel.[27]

Eizenstat also urged both Jewish Americans and state governments to increase their economic investments and to enter into joint enterprises with Israel. He further recommended that Jewish Americans continue to "lobby the Congress and the Administration for the security assistance and economic aid Israel needs."[28] But perhaps most confounding was Eizenstat's counsel to Jewish Americans that "As parents we can make aliyah [immigration to Israel] an acceptable alternative for our children."[29] No Arab American, or perhaps any other member of an ethnic group, could make a similar observation about immigrating to another country and continue to hold a government position on any level. This acceptance, even encouragement, of multiplicity of national loyalty is in marked contrast to Arab Americans who are constantly questioned regarding their "Americanness," and who in reaction to probable negative repercussions have frequently downplayed or denied their ethnic identities. Hence top-ranking politicians and officials of Arab American heritage such as John Mitchell, John Sununu and Philip Habib publicly emphasized their abiding national commitment only to the United States.

A presence of sympathizers in the White House and other top level government bureaus gives the pro-Israel lobby a considerable advantage. In particular, liaison officers are often appointed on the basis of their close personal contacts with the Jewish community or are recruited by Zionist lobby organizations, think tanks, or interest groups. These liaison officers not only arrange meetings and roundtables with the president and other officials,[30] but they also pass on information to Jewish American organizations so that they can tailor their political efforts to specific government concerns.

Alfred H. Moses, Special Adviser to Carter, frankly admitted to a leading Jewish American activist,

I am here primarily to listen to what you and others have to say and to try to be a positive influence in those areas which concern you and me the most. I rely heavily on friends like you to make certain that I am staying in touch with Jewish leadership.[31]

Another White House liaison officer went so far as to recommend the release of advanced technological material on the F-18 plane as a way to "break the ice"[32] with Israeli leaders. These openly pro-Israeli stances are partially a result of personal affiliations, but are also predicated on hard assessments of domestic politics.

Consequently, presidential meetings with leaders of the Jewish American community, long a regular feature of domestic politics, are usually extremely cordial.[33] As with all White House meetings, presidential staffs carefully stage manage these events, determining not only a rigid time schedule, but precisely when and if the president is to appear and if there is to be a "photo opportunity." Jewish American leaders invariably come well prepared and present a coordinated program, often requesting specific financial and military aid packages for Israel. These requests are made in conjunction with identical demands from the Israeli government. In spite of internal divisions, Jewish American groups usually reach a consensus on issues involving Israel. They present, at least in public, a united front. This united front, an enormous asset for lobby efforts,[34] means they can promise and usually deliver a bloc vote for specific candidates or proposals and provide campaign contributions, often through Political Action Committees.

POLITICAL ACTION COMMITTEES

Political Action Committees (PACS) give to both parties across ideological lines, but usually give more money to the party in power.[35] During the 1980s, election laws restricted spending on presidential races, but the House and Senate remained privately funded with no spending limits. Candidates relied heavily on PACs for financial support. The input of PACs on specific legislation is likely to be greatest during the complex committee stages of the legislative process. For the all-important appropriation bills, proposals go through a two-track process. Foreign aid proposals are submitted to the appropriate committees in both the House and Senate and must pass through both the authorization phase, in which the appropriate guidelines are established, and the authorization phase, in which actual amounts are determined. As the two houses invariably present different drafts, a conference committee of members from both houses meets to draft a compromise bill for each phase. After the House and Senate have passed identical versions, the bills are then voted on to be submitted to the president for final approval.[36] The input and influence of staff members during this lengthy and often contentious process is substantial and lobbyists or financial contributors to representatives often use this to their advantage.

Single issue PACs, such as pro-Israeli ones, are the most effective and best funded.[37] Some Jewish Americans believe that their PACs should focus solely on Israel, while others have argued in favor of a broader base of interests . But it is much easier to mobilize support around one well-defined issue. Encouraged by AIPAC, which is not a political action committee, and which seeks a low profile with regard to involvement with PACs, pro-Israeli PACs have names with no visible connection to Israel/Zionism/Jews. The largest include: Citizens Organized PAC, Washington PAC, Joint Action Committee, also Garden State PAC, or Heartland PAC, Maryland Association for Concerned Citizens PAC. From the 1970s to 1980s, pro-Israeli PACs grew exponentially with their financial contributions reaching $3.8 million by the mid-1980s.[38] Ten years later there were 61 pro-Israeli PACs that donated almost $3 million to candidates in a single election year. From 1990 to 2004, pro-Israeli PACs gave an estimated $41.3 to federal candidates and political parties.[39] By 2003 the number of pro-Israeli PACs grew to over 100 and, with private donations by Jewish Americans, totaled as high as $25 million in the 1996 election alone. These PACs focus on a few specific election races to maximize their impacts. They donate to friends of Israel or to candidates running against someone who is considered an "enemy," for example Paul Findley.[40]

In 1988, a group of former government officials, including George W. Ball (former Under Secretary of State) Ambassadors James E. Akins and Andrew I. Killgore and Rear Admiral Robert Hanks, filed a complaint that AIPAC should be considered a PAC, asserting that AIPAC created pro-Israeli PACs and channeled money through board members to PACs. The case revealed that Elizabeth Schrayer, AIPAC's political director, had written a memorandum telling a subordinate where to direct political contributions, an illegal act under federal law. This "smoking gun" evidence was vigorously denied by AIPAC. The case languished until complainants demanded in 1992 that the Federal Election Commission make a decision; the commission had earlier exempted AIPAC from reporting details of income and expenditures. Although AIPAC was still not considered a PAC under electoral regulations, the U.S. District Court of Appeals ruled that the Federal Election Commission re-examine the AIPAC exemption regarding financial disclosures. Again, AIPAC strenuously denied any wrongdoing. Officers testified that AIPAC did not endorse specific candidates or raise funds for them but did refer inquiries to Jewish leaders in specific states or districts. As AIPAC Executive Director, Amitay had vigorously opposed AIPAC involvement with PACS, but once he left office he organized a major pro-Israeli PAC, innocuously named "Washington PAC."

The success of pro-Israeli PACs is a sensitive issue for Zionist supporters as well as politicians. If the American public were to perceive PACs as exercising undue influence on the legislative process, a backlash against all PACs could result. Consequently, AIPAC has recommended using their influence "with measured discretion,"[41] or risk incurring negative fallout. In particular, AIPAC does not want to imperil the flow of foreign and military aid for Israel that Congressional support has hitherto ensured.

CONGRESSIONAL SUPPORT AND FINANCIAL AID

Congress's pro-Israeli sympathies have assured a steady flow of foreign aid to Israel, in spite of opposition by the U.S. public to foreign aid for any nation. Although fully 75 percent of the American public thinks the U.S. spends too much on foreign aid, Congress consistently passes aid bills for Israel that provide the full amount requested by Israel, or sometimes in excess of what the president has requested.[42] In the 1970s when Congress was cutting spending on domestic programs and other foreign aid, appropriations for Israel was 8.7 percent more than the president had requested.[43]

Since the end of the Cold War, U.S. foreign military and economic assistance has declined but aid to Israel has continued to rise. The 2003 occupation of Iraq will skew these overall expenditure trends to some extent. Since the 1980s Israel and Egypt have each received at least $3 billion per annum, or over 40 percent of all U.S. foreign aid, leaving the other 60 percent for the remaining 200-plus nations of the world.[44] Given Egypt's far greater population this is equivalent to $52 per Egyptian and about $14,000 per Israeli. Egypt's per capita income is $1,470 and Israel's is $16,710; Egypt ranks 118 and Israel 37 (high income) among per capita incomes.[45] These figures thereby refute the prevailing myth held by the U.S. public that foreign aid goes to the poorest nations. The aid for Egypt, tied to specific projects, is a strategic weapon that helps to ensure the continuation of the "cold peace" between Egypt and Israel, as well as Egypt's backing for U.S. policies in the region. While aid for Israel certainly has a strategic purpose, the amounts and manner in which they are given demonstrate the success of pro-Israeli lobbying efforts over a number of decades.

During the 1990s U.S. aid to Israel was at least $3 billion per year, $1.2 billion in economic aid and $1.8 billion in military grants.[46] This was more than the amount for all of sub-Saharan Africa, Latin America and the Caribbean. Israel is also the beneficiary of a number of special arrangements. Israel receives U.S. aid at the beginning of each fiscal year in a lump sum that is deposited directly into the Federal Reserve Bank where it earns interest at about 8 percent. Israel is the only nation with this special privilege; other countries receive their grants quarterly and they are carefully overseen by the U.S. government. This privilege is the result of an initiative by Senators Daniel Inouye (D-Hawaii) and Bob Kasten Jr. (R-Wisconsin) in the 1980s. Israel is also protected against any possible cuts in the future by the so-called Cranston amendment (Alan Cranston, D-California) whereby economic aid to Israel will be at least as much as its annual debt payments to the United States. No other nation has such assurances. Unlike regulations governing aid expenditures for other nations, there are also no special restrictions on how Israel spends the money. The U.S. also has arrangements for cooperating in research development with Israel.

Whereas the Saudis and other oil-rich governments pay cash for arms purchases, and even these are strongly opposed in the House and Senate, Israeli purchases are billed to the Israeli trust fund, financed by the Pentagon with U.S. tax dollars. In the 1990s Congress also proposed granting Israel $10 billion in loan guarantees to be given at $2 billion per year for five years. When President George Bush tried to delay the deal in order to pressure the Shamir government to negotiate over the Occupied Territories and to reach a compromise with the Palestinians, Congress balked and pushed ahead. Only the threat of a presidential veto forced Congress to postpone the guarantees for a mere four months and the guarantees went into effect in 1992 with the proviso that the monies were not be used in the West Bank or Gaza. Cognizant of their almost total support in Congress, Israeli governments have little or no incentive to compromise with U.S. presidents who might wish to alter policies regarding Israel and the Palestinians.

At a time when Congress was calling for financial cutbacks, the 2003 budget provided $1 billion in military grants and $9 billion for loan guarantees over four years for Israel. That exceeded the Israeli request for $8 billion, but was less that the $4 billion requested in military grants.

As a direct result of Congressional support, U.S. aid to Israel from 1948 to 2001 totaled over $91 billion and by 2003 the total U.S. financial aid, including special advantages/indirect costs, was estimated to be as high as $1.8 trillion.[47] These amounts do not include the tax exemptions granted for the purchase of Israeli bonds or tax exempt organizations sending assistance to Israel. In large measure owing to the successes of pro-Israeli lobby forces, Israel has been the single largest recipient of U.S. foreign aid since World War II.

It has also benefited from fulsome Congressional backing for its positions on declaring Jerusalem the capital of the state, condemning the PLO and other Palestinian supporters and organizations as terrorists, and a host of other positions involving not only Israel and the Palestinians, but the Arab world as a whole. For example, Congress overwhelmingly (407:9) endorsed Sharon's unilateral plan for a withdrawal from the Gaza Strip in 2004. In a single stroke, Congress thereby abandoned the decades-old policy to support a compromise on the Arab Israeli conflict based on the 1967 UN Resolution 242 and 1993 Oslo agreement. All presidents must take the hard realities of pro-Israeli support in Congress into account when assessing and formulating foreign policy for the region.

8
Act One: The Ford Administration

President Ford came to office with an impeccable pro-Israeli history. Because he had many years of experience in national government and was personally acquainted with many members of Congress, Ford had an advantage in dealing with pressures from both the legislative branch and the public. With his "hands off" approach to the presidency, Ford seemed to have placed particular importance on personal contacts. As documents show, Ford was proactive in dealing with Congress where he felt at home, but in matters of foreign policy Ford took a secondary role to Kissinger's lead. Kissinger had full rein to display his much-touted diplomatic virtuosity. During his first year in office, Ford canvassed leading opinion-makers for their views on the Middle East and met personally with conservative and pro-Israeli spokespersons, included Irving Kristol (a conservative commentator and champion of Israel); former Ambassador and Supreme Court Justice, Arthur Goldberg; Chairman of the Music Corporation of America, R. Wasserman; former Senator William Fulbright and former Under Secretaries of State, George W. Ball and Eugene Rostow.[1] As this list suggests, Ford was interested in gathering opinions and "fresh ideas,"[2] but, with the exception of George Ball and Fulbright, none of those canvassed could be described as neutral or pro-Arab on issues pertaining to the Middle East. Rostow even wrote that he feared Ford was considering offering peace in exchange for the 1967 borders. Rostow recommended that there be no Israeli withdrawal until after a peace settlement had been reached.[3] After his meeting with Ford, Kristol also took it upon himself to recommend a number of people for positions within the administration.

Outside government circles, the industrialist Max Fisher, Ford's old friend from Michigan, played an important role in matters pertaining to Israel. From 1974 through December 1976, Ford met with Fisher over two dozen times and talked to him on the telephone on a regular basis. In addition, Fisher, a leading light in the Republican party, met with other key officials in the White House.[4] Fisher was known to have been a "confidant of several presidents."[5]

On the domestic front, Ford and his advisers consulted Fisher about Jewish American organizations and Fisher periodically recommended that Ford meet with specific individuals. He also made suggestions as to who should be invited to White House functions involving Israel. The Israeli embassy made similar recommendations.[6]

In his special role, Fisher acted as an intermediary between Israeli Labor party leaders and the White House. A strong supporter of the Labor party, Fisher discouraged direct contacts with pro-Likud organizations and the extremist Jewish Defense League (JDL). He questioned whether Vice President Nelson Rockefeller should attend a conference of the Zionist Organization of America (ZOA) which had taken a hard line pro-Likud stance. Rockefeller was subsequently asked to attend the conference to encourage a softer ZOA line.[7] During Reagan's and the second Bush administrations, the anti-Likud opposition was dropped and the Republican party established mutually cordial alliances with the Likud.

Ford also used Fisher's good offices to send "behind the scenes" messages to Israel. Before Fisher's summer 1976 trip to Israel, the NSC suggested that he reassured the Israelis as to Ford's policies and kept them informed as to public opinion in the U.S. The NSC wanted Fisher to:

Reassure the Israelis that there is *no change contemplated in our basic policy* [emphasis in original]. He could also suggest that by making major issues out of minor incidents, the Israeli's *tend to hurt their own image* [emphasis in original] in this country where there is considerable public and even Congressional sentiment for trying to find a means of dealing with the Palestinians without in any way compromising Israel's security.[8]

In return, Fisher talked with Ford and Scowcroft about his strong opposition to the PLO, the Arab Boycott, the U.N. Resolution equating Zionism and racism and any visits by PLO officials to the U.S. He also urged an increase in the aid package for Israel.[9] For his efforts, Fisher was described by Ford as "an unofficial ambassador between the United States and Israel."[10]

However, Fisher's prominent role sometimes provoked negative reviews. After Fisher and a number of other Jewish Americans publicly protested the sale of planes to Egypt in 1976, Ambassador George Feldman called to complain. Believing the protest was misguided, Feldman recommended that the White house should "remind Max Fisher that we had a very difficult time getting Egypt out of the clutches of the Soviets and it is to Israel's advantage that we did ..."[11] Realizing that it would be awkward for Ford to reproach Fisher,

Feldman suggested that someone in the State or Defense Departments could issue the rebuff.

Given his close relationships with Zionist organizations and individual Jewish Americans, Ford was surprised by the vehemence of opposition from pro-Israeli forces in Congress and Jewish American organizations to his announced "reassessment" of Middle East policy. Although the Democrats had a majority in both the House and Senate, Congressional support for Israel cut across partisan lines and even Ford could not always stem the tide of opposition to his policies regarding either the Arab Israeli conflict or, as has been described, Cyprus.

From the outset, the Ford White House received a steady stream of letters and communications on a wide range of issues of concern to Israel and Jewish Americans. Two major letter campaigns focused on the status of Soviet and Syrian Jews and others dealt with increasing U.S. foreign and military aid to Israel.[12] Jewish American organizations also protested the sale of arms, however minor, to any Arab nation.[13]

Similar objections were lodged against the PLO and any U.S. contact with it. Letters poured in opposing Arafat's visit to the United Nations in 1974 and against the opening of a PLO office in Washington in 1976. The White House consistently stressed that neither Ford nor Secretary of State Kissinger would deal with the PLO as long as it did not recognize "Israel's right to exist."[14]

Relations with the PLO became a political "hot potato" when the Americans were evacuated from the Lebanon in summer 1976 following the assassination of the U.S. ambassador, Francis Melloy, Jr., which Washington claimed did not involve groups associated with the PLO. After a careful assessment of the various options for the evacuation, the sea route was selected as the least dangerous, assuming a "permissive environment."[15] The unsung subtext of this was that it necessitated the assistance of the PLO who, at that point, controlled the security in West Beirut. The PLO was more than willing to assist, but it did not get the credit it undoubtedly hoped would accrue from its protection of American lives. Fearing a backlash from the Zionist lobby, Washington did everything possible to downplay Palestinian involvement and did not publicly applaud its assistance. Press Secretary Ron Nessen was told not to mention the PLO specifically and that if asked about assurances of safety from the PLO to respond and (only IF PRESSED [emphasis in original]:

These assurances were received thru third parties including the Palestinians among others. As to whether the President's remarks enhance the position of the PLO, I would say that you have to look at this operation as basically humanitarian with a dangerous situation on the ground.[16]

The Ford camp so feared even this minimal contact with the PLO in the Lebanon that it prepared a full disclaimer for the 1976 election campaign with the often repeated refrain that "the question of recognition and negotiations with the PLO does not arise as long as the PLO does not recognize the existence of the state of Israel and accept Resolutions 242 and 338 ... This remains our policy."[17]

But negative responses from Congress were even more damaging to Ford and Kissinger's attempts to shift the direction of foreign policy. Israel interpreted the reassessment period as a not-so-veiled attempt to force it to make concessions to the Arabs that it found unacceptable. Israel made its displeasure known to the White House through its Washington embassy and Jewish American lobby groups. They immediately rushed on stage to bring domestic political pressure to bear. Early in Ford's term, 71 senators sent him a joint letter in opposition to the PLO and its growing presence at the United Nations. Ford sent personal letters to each signatory stressing that the U.S. continued to oppose the presence of the PLO at the United Nations.[18]

Then in the summer of 1975, responding "favorably to an AIPAC initiative",[19] 76 senators (75 percent of the Senate) issued a strongly worded public letter in favor of aid to Israel. Members of Congress as well as state and local officials supported this letter. As it was meant to do, the letter attracted media attention and became a stumbling block to improved relations with Arab governments.[20] As with the earlier Senate letter, Ford responded to each signatory, writing a personal thank you note to "Chuck" Percy for his help in attempts to alter Middle East policy.[21]

These Senate letters demonstrated the ability of the Zionist lobby to rally forces on all levels of local and national government in favor of Israel. They were also a public warning to Ford about the strength of the lobby and of the potentially dire political consequences of upstaging or sidelining it. All administrations must consider Congressional support for Israel. Any moves that are construed as harmful to Israeli interests, or in favor of the Arabs, cause vocal and vociferous opposition. Consequently, most administrations and individual politicians prefer to steer clear of accepting any role in peace-making or foreign policy that might have negative impacts on their bids for reelection. These public displays of support for Israel upstaged the Ford administration's attempts to persuade Israel to make the concessions necessary to reach any settlement with the Arabs. It also impeded efforts to convince Arab regimes that Washington was sincere in its desire for a more even-handed approach that would, at least in some measure, address their major demands.[22] This is a clear example of the pro-Israeli lobby's success in mobilizing enough domestic political support, especially in Congress, to stop U.S. policy overtures that Israel opposes.

In reaction to this political crescendo, Arab governments expressed both their concern and appreciation for Ford's attempts to improve relations. However, these expressions of support scarcely compensated for the massive public and political sympathy for Israel. Nor did the obvious pro-Israeli stance in Congress encourage Arab leaders, even those who were anxious for rapprochement, to depend on U.S. assurances that it would act in the role of a neutral mediator.

SADAT AND THE SINAI DISENGAGEMENT AGREEMENTS

Attempts to bring Sadat and Egypt on to the U.S. stage brought these conflicting policies into the spotlight. As Kissinger made clear, these moves were intended to bolster the U.S. role in the region and in no way detracted from Israeli strength or U.S. commitment to it. They were aimed to enable

> the United States and Israel to continue to control the negotiating process, keeping Soviet influence at a low level in the Middle East, and allowing Sadat and other Arab moderate leaders [read pro-U.S.] to dominate the radicals [read PLO, Syria and Iraq] and continue to work for a peaceful settlement with recognition of Israel and its right to live in peace.[23]

By the spring of 1975 the White House feared an impending war in the Middle East begun by Israel. Kissinger did not view such a war as in the best interests of the U.S. and was anxious to keep control of the peace process so as to avoid any international forum that was not controlled by the United States. Kissinger believed this approach to be in the best interests of Israel as well.[24] Israeli leaders were skeptical; they wanted a settlement but on their own terms with few compromises. Israel knew that the balance of power was in its favor and that with its "lock" on Congress there was little likelihood it would be forced into positions it did not want to take. Simply, the Ford administration did not have the political clout or perhaps even the will to pressure Israel to accept its demands even though the U.S. libretto did not include a Palestinian state or, indeed, any direct Palestinian involvement.

Consequently, Congressional opposition to Egypt and Sadat continued even in the face of the obvious willingness of the Egyptian government to move out of the Soviet sphere of influence and to alter long-held policies domestically and with regard to Israel. Part of Kissinger's grand scheme was to wrest Egypt away from Soviets and to start a step-by-step process controlled by United States. U.S. Egyptian links were further forged by a personal meeting between Sadat and Ford during the president's trip to Salzburg in summer 1975. The Ford administration was disappointed with Israel's reluctance to compromise, but it had little leverage to force it to do so.

Ford's performance faced a cold reception in Congress and the media. When long-time Speaker of the House Carl Albert (D-Oklahoma), spoke in favor of Ford's policies toward Egypt he was personally abused by a Congressional colleague.[25]

The overt hostility to Sadat and the Arabs became a public problem when Sadat visited the U.S. in 1975. The trip had been arranged to take place after the signing of the Sinai disengagement agreement, a major victory for U.S. aims in the region and a considerable political risk for Sadat. Traveling with a fairly large entourage for maximum publicity at home, Sadat portrayed the visit as a gain for Egypt because its new alliance with the U.S. would result in financial assistance to alleviate Egypt's dire economic straits. The White House was eager for Sadat to be warmly welcomed and to be treated with respect. Negative reviews of the visit by Congress and the media was of great concern to the White House. Ambassador Eilts summarized the problem to Ron Nessen:

> ... Sadat was and is the key element in turning situation around and his visit to United States deserves to be personl [sic] triumph and tribute to his statesmanship. U.S. media in any case, will I assume require no urging to focus on President and Mrs. Sadat's activities and personalities. We are confident they will make a highly favorable impact.[26]

Eilts added that the Arabs felt that Sadat had sold out and that the Syrians and Palestinians, in particular, viewed the visit as the "payoff."

To off-set these perceptions, Eilts urged Nessen to portray the visit not only as a tribute to Sadat, but to Egypt as a nation.

As the Sadat visit approached, the Ford administration went into damage control. Ford suggested sending Vice President Nelson Rockefeller, who had been "a bit upset" about his perpetual understudy role, along with Sadat on the entire trip. Making no secret of his disdain for the Vice President, Kissinger enthused, "It would flatter Sadat out of his mind."[27]

But in spite of White House efforts, Sadat was publicly rebuffed by New York Mayor Abraham Beame, who chose to play to his large Jewish constituency rather than to further the best interests of U.S. foreign policy. Ironically, the staunchly pro-Democratic Mayor Richard Daley of Chicago gave Sadat the welcome that had been denied by New York City.[28]

While touring the Middle East some Congressmen did become uncomfortable with the Israeli hard sell.

> There was some resentment toward the propaganda type approach that was used on the delegation ... we got the definite impression that the Israelis would like to introduce an American presence, whether civilian or military in Israel – a step many members view with trepidation.[29]

Sadat did his utmost to charm these same Congressional delegates into modifying their anti-Egyptian views. He made an impressive plea for peace and the coordination of Egypt and U.S. interests, but made no mention of the Palestinians. During this trip, he posed for photos, even with junior staff members, and played the role of the gracious host. The Congressional reaction was that Sadat was a

> genuine, straightforward world leader of imposing stature. They were most reassured by his candid views and expressed desire for peace, in contrast to the carefully orchestrated Israeli propaganda approach and the stolidly militant aura of that nation. However, I doubt that many of them will be very vocal in their assessment for fear of the Jewish reaction back home.[30]

As predicted, although some representatives may have privately altered their views of Israel and Egypt, the shifts were not apparent in Congress where opposition to rapprochement with Egypt remained strong.

To push for approval of the Sinai Agreement, Ford met with the Senate Wednesday Club, composed of key senators.[31] The Second

Sinai Agreement (1 September 1975) was a complex arrangement for the partial withdrawal from Sinai by Israeli troops, the establishment of buffer zones followed by an early warning system in Sinai that involved the deployment of U.S. civilians, not to exceed 200 personnel, to oversee the process.[32] Reactions to this agreement and the deployment of U.S. personnel were mixed.

In his usual blunt and colorful way, Wayne Hays (D-Ohio), a long-term Congressman, bellowed:

> ... I can't say what those crazy bastards up there [on the Hill] will say. I don't think there will be a bad reaction to the use of civilian personnel. If there is any criticism it will be muted on the Hill because of the Israeli involvement. You will not get the same kind of reaction that you got ... on Turkish aid situation.[33]

Because the Sinai agreement was a sensitive political issue, the White House kept close track of the responses to it and tallied the numbers of positive versus negative comments. Israel and the Zionist lobby only signed on to the Sinai agreement after the U.S. agreed to an American Israeli Memorandum of Understanding that stipulated that the U.S. respond to Israel's "military, economic and energy needs." Thus, on 8 September 1975, Ford had a special briefing session with a delegation of Jewish American leaders led by Max Fisher at the White House. Many of these leaders had communicated with the White House just days before the meeting and Fisher met privately with Ford and Kissinger to coordinate the script for the event. Although the Zionist lobby had been extremely wary of the Sinai Agreement, once it and the Memorandum of Understanding were in place, they were fulsome in congratulations and flooded the White house with telephone calls, wires and letters.[34] The Zionist lobby recognizes that as performers politicians crave public recognition and seek, if not standing ovations, at least respectful applause.

But in spite of the administration's hard work to improve relations with Egypt, Congress still passed a resolution opposing arms sales to Egypt in spring 1976.[35] There were no coordinated attempts to mobilize Arab Americans before or after the Sinai Agreements. They were not part of the political cast. The political climate in the United States exacerbated Sadat's vulnerability in Egypt and the rest of the Arab world, where many opposed his policies. As Scowcroft explained, "Sadat is taking much flak from the Arab world. Delay in

Congress gives Sadat detractors ammunition that the agreement is a lousy one."[36]

Congressional opposition also made it difficult for Ford, particularly in an election year, to take steps toward a negotiated settlement that was not based solely on Israeli demands. Fully cognizant of these political realities, Israel refused to sign the Sinai Agreement (or any others) until Congress gave its approval, and Congress would only ratify after Israel and/or the Zionist lobby had given their assent. This has made a workable peace treaty to resolve the Arab Israeli conflict impossible. The same dynamic continues to the present day.

Senator Fulbright focused on this paradox in a speech before the Middle East Institute on 3 October 1975.

> ... the key to a Middle East peace is in the internal politics of this country. As long as the Israeli lobby retains its extraordinary power to mobilize large majorities in Congress, the executive will be hobbled in any efforts to achieve a peace based on Security Council Resolution 242.[37]

The Zionist lobby has been careful to downplay its influence in Congress. Over the past six decades it has characterized Israeli and U.S. interests as mutually complimentary. During the Ford administration, the well-known Israeli champion, Norman Podhoretz, detailed this position in a letter to a White House aide.

> And as for Congress, I can tell you from personal experience, on the basis of 25 years in Congress, that support of the State of Israel in the Congress of the United States is not the result of pressure from any group. It stems from the conviction that the continued survival and well being of Israel is in the long-range interests of the United States, and fully in accord with the spiritual and political principles that we sustain and that sustain us as a nation.[38]

After 9/11, with neo-conservatives and the Christian right in the ascendancy in Washington, the appeals to religious affiliations have particular resonance for many U.S. politicians and citizens.

Egypt was a major financial beneficiary of the Sinai Agreement, but Israel's reluctant participation in the Sinai Agreement also resulted in an economic pay off for it. In fact, Israel was set to receive $2.3 billion in U.S. aid in 1976, compared with $700 million for Egypt. "Israel was so confident of them she included them in her printed budget prior to the Sinai Agreement ... The $2.3 billion for Israel would have been necessary with or without the Sinai Agreement."[39]

Senators then actually pushed Ford to increase budget allotments for Israel. To which Ford asked, "Without my making any promises or commitments here, tell me what is the figure you really want for ... Israel?"[40] They responded "$320 million." Ford waffled but he was not likely to reject these demands, particularly in an election year. One Ford aide sang out that, "this Administration is not going to jeopardize Israel's security on the basis of budget austerity. Our argument is only over what levels are really required for Israel's security and what represents adequate assistance to meet Israel's real needs."[41] But Israel and its supporters consistently asked for increases to the aid package, pegging requests to be equal or more than that received by all the Arab states.

Divas and star performers always want better roles, the best arias and more stage time. There is similar competition in the world of diplomatic exchanges. The Zionist lobby carefully tracks how often Arab leaders are received in Washington and what sort of hospitality or "state visits" is proffered, demanding "equal time" and treatment for Israeli leaders and visitors. Reacting to these demands, Ford made certain that Yitzhak Rabin was given star treatment during his March 1976 visit to Washington. The state dinner for Rabin, at which the guest list was a virtual "who's who" of Jewish Americans, was a "glittering"[42] affair. It was followed in May by a then-unprecedented briefing of leading Jewish Americans at the Pentagon; these have since become fairly common.

In election years, White House officials make concerted efforts to keep in touch with ethnic voters and organizations. Under Ford, William Baroody, the Assistant to the President for Public Liaison, visited with the largest Jewish donors to the Republican party during a swing trip to the west.[43] Keeping the pulse of Jewish American communities, Fisher was also useful in gauging political support for Ford in the 1976 election.

Aware of the political potential of Jewish Americans, the White House invited 150 American Jewish leaders to meet with the President and Mrs. Ford in September 1976. During this meeting, chaired by Max Fisher, Ford stressed his support for Israel and the massive $4.3 billion in aid in two budgets (40 percent of all Israeli aid since 1948 was appropriated under the Ford administration).[44] Earlier about half the group had attended a workshop to discuss election tactics to ensure a high Jewish vote for Ford and to gain a Republican victory in the presidential election. The Ford committee aimed at target states, with substantial Jewish populations where a high Jewish voter turn out could make a difference in the election. The committee also sought public support from religious and business leaders.

A full time liaison, David Lissy, was hired to place ads in Jewish newspapers, prepare responses for questions most likely to be of concern to Jewish Americans, to arrange meetings between Ford and key "image makers" and to organize a major press conference where the President could focus on issues of concern to the community.[45] Fisher encouraged meetings with Jewish leaders in the key target cities in the states with high electoral votes or where there had been a marginal differential in the 1972 election. Noting that most Jewish Americans placed Israel as the number one issue of concern, Ford was coached to stress that the "U.S. will not pressure Israel to make one-sided concessions."[46] But the Carter campaign used Ford's performances during the Cyprus crisis and the anti-Arab Boycott campaign to upstage and outmaneuver the president. As the next chapter reveals, the major "production" of the anti-Arab Boycott campaign demonstrates how lobbies influence foreign policy and effect political outcomes.

9
A Major Production:
The Arab Boycott Campaign

To understand the anti-boycott campaign and its impact a bit of history is necessary. The League of Arab States initiated the Arab Boycott against products of Jewish industry in Palestine in late 1945 as part of the Arab nationalist struggle against the Zionist endeavor to establish an independent Jewish state in Palestine. The so-called primary boycott tried to prevent the import of products into Arab states from Jewish manufacturers in Palestine. In 1951 following the establishment of the state of Israel and the losses in the 1948 war, a secondary boycott to deter third parties from contributing to the Israeli economy was enacted. The secondary boycott attempted to use well established and, under international law, legal economic means to limit and weaken economic growth of an enemy nation, in this case Israel. Although armistices were ultimately signed between Israel and the belligerent Arab states following the 1948 war, without formal peace treaties a state of war technically still existed. Thus under the secondary boycott it was illegal for any Arab state to engage in economic trade or transactions with Israel; third party companies who had businesses in Israel were also banned from trading or establishing production facilities in Arab states. The Arab League through the permanent Central Office based in Damascus kept a so-called blacklist for the boycott of Israel. This office kept track and publicized those firms and businesses with economic relations with Israel. The terms and regulations governing the boycott were amended and enlarged upon several times by the League during the 1970s; however, actual enforcement of the boycott and compliance with blacklist was left to the individual Arab states.

In practice, the implementation of the boycott was a haphazard affair. The boycott had some limited success in pressuring some European based firms and states, particularly in Eastern Europe, to refrain from economic exchanges and business with Israel. The boycott's impact in the United States was best known for the embarrassing and, in terms of impact on Israel, totally useless blacklisting of Hollywood stars such as Elizabeth Taylor and Barbra Streisand. Even the Arab actor Omar Sharif was blacklisted for appearing with the latter in a Hollywood film. Arab governments stressed that the boycott was directed against Israel, and was not implemented against Americans or Jews elsewhere. Reports on the boycott seem to validate that contention. Between 1970 and 1975 barely two dozen requests based on religion or ethnicity were reported out of 50,000 boycott request reports.[1] Other Arab nations, for example Syria, would take specific firms off the blacklist if they invested in Syria.[2] Saudi Arabia, although it did have religiously based entry restrictions, had business relations with Jewish companies and businesspersons. Thus the impact of the boycott in the United States was minimal.

However, the oil boom prices of the 1970s led Israel to fear that the increase of Arab economic clout could make the boycott a more effective weapon. US officials estimated exports to the Arab world at $3.3 billion in 1974, nearly double the $1.7 billion in 1973. They estimated exports would reach $5 billion in 1975 and a huge $10 billion in 1980.[3] Actually, OPEC investments in the United States reached $5.5 billion in 1975.[4] These exports represented between 200,000 and 350,000 American jobs.[5] Most of the export value was based on consulting, engineering, and contracting services. As a result of these massive investments, it was a distinct possibility that Arab governments might increase the pressure on firms not to do business with Israel. They might also threaten companies that if they continued contacts with Israel, the burgeoning Arab market would be closed to them.

The campaign against the Arab Boycott had all the characteristics of a major operatic production, complete with star power, a forceful script and music, directors, chorus, and elaborate stage set. With a detailed libretto and production schedule, the pro-Israeli and Zionist forces within the United States launched a full-scale attack against the Arab Boycott and any compliance by the United States or U.S. businesses in 1975. The campaign was clearly timed to coincide with the forthcoming 1976 presidential elections, attaining a full crescendo in the crucial election year. In contrast, the Arab forces and their allies within the U.S. had no script or timetable and were left to scurry around backstage, ad libbing whenever they appeared. In the case of the anti-Arab Boycott the Zionist lobby and pressure groups utilized all the techniques described in Chapter 4; these included letter campaigns, personal visits to legislatures and officials on state and national levels, organized group pressure, publicity campaigns, media blitzes and a full array of legislative and legal moves to enact new laws against any compliance with the boycott. These techniques were coordinated and developed into national and local productions.

The Israeli government was a driving force – albeit off-stage – behind the anti-boycott campaign in the United States. U.S. government officials summarized Israel's position as follows:

> Israel views relaxation of boycott enforcement as an important element in the Arab-Israeli peacemaking process. A combination of events – domestic economic difficulties, the slowdown of the world economy and the sudden affluence of the Arab markets – apparently has convinced senior Israeli officials that action must be taken to weaken the boycott. The focus of this effort is on measures to prevent US firms from complying with boycott-related requests ... Israeli officials are aware of the official U.S. anti-boycott legislation. They do not appear concerned that efforts to force changes in boycott enforcement may interfere with U.S.–Arab relations with resulting damage to U.S. mediating efforts.[6]

Thus, in conjunction with Israeli foreign policy directives, pro-Israeli groups in the United States began attacking the Arab Boycott on national and local levels in 1975.[7] The anti-boycott campaign was primarily directed against the secondary boycott and American compliance with it.[8] It is not the purpose here to provide a full account of the campaign against the Arab Boycott – much of which was waged through proposed legislation for more rigorous laws governing compliance by private U.S. businesses. However, even a brief review of the performance, or campaign, illustrates the political potential of concerted, well-organized lobby campaigns. The campaign sought to publicize the anti-Israeli and allegedly anti-Semitic nature of the Arab Boycott and successfully forced the enactment of new legislation against any U.S. compliance with it.

Using the media, letter writing campaigns, and most crucially, legislative changes enacted by Congress and state legislatures, the anti-boycott campaigners put extensively personal pressure on a multitude of elected officials including both Presidents Ford and Carter

The opening notes of the campaign were sounded after the Senate Committee on Foreign Relations published the names of over 1,500 U.S. corporations on the blacklist in February 1975. The list was erroneously categorized as the Saudi Arabian blacklist, not the Arab League list. At the same time, the committee also published the lengthy terms governing the boycott. Within weeks, the Anti-Defamation League of B'nai B'rith (the ADL was established in 1913 to fight anti-Semitism in the U.S. under the umbrella of the B'nai B'rith, the Jewish fraternal organization formed in 1843/44) launched a massive publicity campaign publicizing the boycott and what it termed the "pattern of bowing" to the boycott by U.S. businesses and banks. In June and July the ADL filed legal charges against specific businesses claiming that they had violated the US Civil Rights Act by complying with the terms of the boycott. Following additional information regarding compliance by specific businesses and federal departments, the ADL escalated the campaign by filing a suit against specific government officials.

Whereas Congress had shown little interest in the boycott over the previous two decades (for example, the boycott was mentioned in the House only once in 1954 and only once in the Senate in 1964), in light of pressure from pro-Israeli interest groups and the publicity campaign about the boycott, Congressional attention grew. In 1975 the boycott was mentioned 46 times, while the 1976 *Congressional Record* index indicated over 70 mentions, including remarks in the House and Senate and articles/comments inserted by members of Congress into the record. This was an easy "feel good" issue in which representatives and senators could garner political support and presumably increased financially donations from pro-Zionist organizations and supporters; nor did they need fear any negative reviews or fallout from voters or from those few individuals or groups that might see the boycott as a legitimate tool in the Palestinian struggle for self determination.

The ADL and other Zionist organizations supplied Congress with lists of firms who allegedly had complied with the boycott. Representatives then called for the banning of foreign investment that required discrimination and labeled the boycott anti-Semitic. Many politicians publicly supported ADL campaigns against the boycott and compliance with it and even went so far as to demand the cessation of all arms sales to Arab states and for surveillance of those dealing with Middle East interests.[9] Bowing to pressure, the House Subcommittee on International Trade and Commerce launched hearings on the boycott. The American Jewish Congress, ADL, and the American Jewish Committee on the Arab Boycott all testified before the committee, arguing forcibly for stronger laws and the enforcement of anti-boycott legislation.[10] The issue had become a political "hot potato".

With his finely tuned political ear, President Ford quickly attempted to quiet the growing fervor. At his 26 February 1975 news conference he firmly stated that discrimination based on religious and ethnic grounds was "contrary to the American tradition and repugnant to American principles." But with mounting Congressional support, the campaign gained momentum. By 1976 – election year – the boycott issue had become a common topic of debate; increasing numbers of representatives and senators joined in the chorus to demand more stringent regulations to prevent compliance with any parts of the boycott and, indeed, pushed for legislation to punish firms or individuals who complied with the boycott.

The Republican administration under Ford was firmly opposed to stricter laws to regulate the compliance of U.S. businesses with the boycott. Although the Ford administration was on record as opposing the boycott and, indeed, as opposing discrimination based on religious, racial or ethnic grounds, it also believed that the "diplomatic approach ... [was] the most effective way to proceed."[11] In his statement before the Subcommittee on International Trade and Commerce, House Foreign Affairs Committee, Sidney Sober, Acting Assistant Secretary for Near Eastern and South Asian Affairs, summarized the impact of the boycott and U.S. policies, regarding it as follows:

> It is our understanding that, generally speaking, the act of trading with Israel – as such – does not violate any of the regulations of the boycott organization ... Arab countries reserve the power to interpret the boycott regulations. they are not uniformly applied. There are a number of firms which do business in Israel and Arab countries ... I want to reemphasize ... that we opposed the boycott and will continue to make our Opposition to it known, and – that we will continue to oppose any efforts to discriminate against American firms or individuals on the basis of religion or ethnic background ... It is our conviction that in the attainment of peace lies the fundamental basis for the resolution of the boycott issue.[12]

An impressive array of government departments, including the National Security Council, Departments of State, Treasury, Commerce and Justice, opposed additional legislation against the boycott. In particular, the CIA reported that the boycott had not affected Israel and was not likely to do so in the future.[13]

Internal White House memos also emphasized that "despite allegations to the contrary, it [the boycott] generally is not applied on religious and ethnic grounds."[14]

Most tellingly, White House advisers recognized "Arab efforts to deny Israel economic advantages of trading with third countries (which, to some extent, are not unlike our own efforts to economically isolate Cuba, North Korea, Vietnam and Cambodia."[15]

The economic ramification of additional legislation was another major concern. Although U.S. trade with the Arab bloc had increased during the 1970s, European or Asian manufacturers, to the detriment of U.S. businesses, could easily replace products from the U.S. Officials worried that

> There is a strong possibility that the Arabs could and would turn toward other sources of supply if the United States were to undertake to prohibit U.S. firms from complying with boycott requests. The U.S. lacks leverage to force the Arabs to retreat on the boycott issue. There is little for which the Arabs are dependent on the U.S., even though we may be their preferred source of supply for many commodities.[16]

When the Ford administration sought to soften anti-Arab boycott stances, pressure for more legislation increased. Numerous states, most notably New York and California, enacted anti-boycott legislation. By September 1975, there were no fewer than 14 bills and two Congressional resolutions before Congress. The White House characterized this legislative onslaught as the "meat-axe approach to dealing with the problem."[17]

The Ford administration attempted to deal with this political "hot potato" by appealing to individual members of Congress and by supporting those bills that appeared to be the least damaging to U.S. interests in the Arab world.[18] The White House staff was instructed to study and to make recommendations on the issue.

As previously noted, the ADL had earlier (June, July) filed suits against several U.S. corporations. In September it filed against Rogers "Doc" Morton, the Secretary of Commerce. This suit alleged that Morton had circulated bid invitations, participation of which was limited by the boycott, and of protecting companies that had complied with the boycott. The ADL demanded that the Commerce Department publicly release the names of all companies that had complied with the boycott. Although the department readily agreed to note U.S. anti-boycott terms on all tenders, it refused under the terms of confidentiality to release specific names. The Morton case is indicative of the dramatic impact of public court cases. In something of a star turn, Morton, an exceedingly reluctant cast member, was called to testify before the Subcommittee on Oversight and Investigations of the House Committee on Interstate and Foreign Commerce on 12 September. White House advisers recommended that Morton should inform the committee that the president had ordered the Commerce Department to amend the regulations of the Export Administration Act along the following lines: prohibiting U.S. companies from complying with boycott requests that were discriminatory, requiring U.S. exporters to report boycott requests, requiring related services, i.e., banks to report compliance with boycott. But when Morton refused to make copies of the reports from private firms doing business in the Arab world public, he was excoriated in the press, and on 11 November the House subcommittee found him in contempt in a vote of ten to five.[19] Within days, 25 Democratic Congressmen filed suit against Morton and against Interior Secretary Thomas Kleppe for hindering implementation of U.S. anti-boycott policies. Faced with this concerted pressure, Morton was forced to back down. In December, with White House acquiescence, he agreed to provide the requested documents.

In performing dramatic roles, divas and leading men have a number of options as to how to play their roles. Similarly, President Ford had a number of options for how to "play" the ongoing drama. Each option posed both pro and con domestic (read political) and international impacts. White House advisers drew up detailed scenarios for each possibility; their recommendations to the president were made largely on the basis of domestic political impacts. One option was essentially to comply with demands for full disclosure and making it mandatory for firms to report any compliance for public inspection. This would obviously defuse political dissension, particularly between Congress and the White House, but it also posed problems of "cheating" by firms in their reports and, more crucially, could force the Arab world to turn elsewhere for goods. Other options entailed continuing to assure the confidentiality of reports or only giving information on specific firms to the appropriate Congressional committees; some tightening up of the process of reporting was also suggested. While these approaches were acceptable to U.S. businesses, they did not satisfy Congressional demands and the White House also worried that Congress might leak hitherto confidential material to the public. It was also suggested that the Commerce Department should prohibit any compliance with the boycott requests, but should keep the names of specific firms who had received such requests confidential. This option to ban any compliance was "what the private groups concerned really want."[20] However, the possible negative impacts of this option were considerable.

- Since the U.S. is the only country with legislation opposing the Arab Boycott, even in principle, foreign firms would not be under similar constraints with regard to full cooperation with Arab boycott requests.
- It would be interpreted by Arab countries as a shift in U.S. foreign policy, which could jeopardize peaceful settlement in the Middle East.
- It would be very difficult to detect compliance with covert Arab boycott requests.[21]

Finally, Ford could recommend limiting "prohibition to boycott requests based on ethnic or religious considerations."[22] This option, although it would not totally satisfy the pro-Israeli groups, was the recommended course of action. It was also recommended that a top level meeting be held including Secretary Kissinger, Brent Scowcroft, Bob Oakley and others, to flesh out a strategy for implementing the decisions and how the changes should be publicized to Congress, U.S. citizens, and Arab nations and Israel. In reaction to the mounting campaign, President Ford announced, on 20 November 1975, three pages of new directives to tighten the implementation of already existing regulatory laws.[23]

The executive branch policy may be summarized as follows:

- end trade promotion based on material with boycott clauses;
- publicize U.S. opposition to the boycott;
- require firms to report responses to boycott requests;
- ban exporters from complying with any requests discriminating on the basis of race, color, religion, sex, or national origin;
- tell U.S. firms that refusal to deal with another party owing to boycott requests might involve antitrust laws;
- take direct action against the (U.S. based) Bechtel Corporation (one of the world's largest engineering, construction and project management corporations with extensive operations in the Arab world), and the Federal Reserve Board to notify banks of U.S. anti-boycott policies.[24]

Although Ford had backtracked and given in to many of the campaigns demands, the anti-boycott forces only escalated their demands. On 28 November, the Anti-Defamation League of B'nai B'rith called the measures "a welcome affirmative step", but they "failed to come to grips with the full scope of Arab boycott operations in the U.S. against Israel."[25]

Just a producers seek to optimize ticket sales and audience size by opening large scale opera productions at favorable times of the year, so too do lobby pressure groups seek to optimize their impact. The timing of the anti-boycott campaign had been well chosen to put maximum pressure on politicians just before a presidential election year. In the hope of gaining possible votes and financial support for campaigns, many Congressmen and other politicians signed on to the anti-boycott legislation. In supporting the campaign they stood to gain considerable financial and public support from pro-Zionist groups and individuals in the U.S. while they risked virtually zero negative political fallout. Thus the Ford administration was in an extremely awkward political position. International and economic interests called for soft pedaling the boycott issue and for trying to promote – behind the scenes – changes in Arab policies. But such moderation was viewed by much of the voting public as bowing to Arab pressure and oil interests – hardly popular actors.

As election year neared, the anti-Arab Boycott chorus increased in volume and intensity. Israel also intensified its campaign against the boycott with the full support of domestic pressure groups in the U.S. U.S. policy-makers knew that Israeli officials are aware of the official U.S. anti-boycott legislation, but that they were not really concerned "that efforts to force changes in boycott enforcement may interfere with U.S.-Arab relations with resulting damage to U.S. mediating efforts."[26]

Fearing the possible political fallout, Ford's advisers placed the issue at the top of the agenda for the first Cabinet meeting in 1976. Schmults led off with a summary of the various actions taken thus far and Kissinger commented on the potential impacts internationally, particularly with regard to the Middle East. Kissinger emphasized that the United States was currently employing boycotts against Cuba, Korea, North Vietnam and selectively against Russia and China. He rhetorically asked what would happen if Great Britain passed a law against U.S. boycotting third countries and noted that these practices could severely damage U.S. relations with Saudi Arabia.[27] Ford ended the discussion by noting that it was a serious issue that would have to be followed closely to strike "that delicate balance needed to protect the varied interests of the United States."[28]

With these considerations in mind, advisers continued to make recommendations regarding the major bills before the House and Senate. In summary, the Stevenson Amendment (Senate Bill) called for reports filed after the enactment of the bill to be made public, and required the Secretary of Commerce to institute regulations barring U.S. businesses from "refusing to do business with any other domestic concern ... for the purpose of enforcing or implementing a restrictive trade practice," but with specific exemptions for banks. In contrast the Bingham–Rosenthal (House Bill) specifically mentioned Israel while the proposed Jewish conference substitute bill also specifically referred to Israel.[29] Following exhaustive research, debate and meetings by State and Treasury officials with various Senators and Representatives, the President was advised to emphasize his opposition to further legislation because of potential damage to wide U.S. interests. However, they noted that,

> Since it is unlikely that the Senate can be stopped, given the head of steam which has built up, we should make our points clearly but quietly in the hopes that the amendments will get buried in the House or dropped in Conference.
>
> If this strategy fails, the President may have to decide between vetoing or accepting a modified version of the Bill. There was no agreement as to what to recommend to the President in this situation – although there was agreement that for the moment the Administration should take a very tough line in the hopes of heading off the necessity for such a choice.[30]

In largely vain attempts to mute the furor, White House liaison officers with the Jewish community met with Jewish leaders and reported that a compromise was possible. Noting the important political ramifications of the anti-boycott campaign and Ford's relations with the Jewish constituency, David Lissy noted:

> There is a growing sense among a broad cross section of the leadership of the Jewish community that there has been too much friction of late between the Administration and the community. It is apparent that the Administration is "winning." A move to reach a compromise on the Stevenson bill is not likely to be seen as a sign of weakness on our part but rather as an expression of interest.

> As we have discussed, there are growing prospects of very substantial support for the President from the Jewish community. You are well aware of the significance of this. We clearly cannot solve our problems on all issues of concern to the community but here is a chance for reasonably modest action not inconsistent with basic Administration policy.[31]

Ford was informed by Scowcroft and Seidman about the ramifications of this issue to his campaign. Providing a detailed description of the pros and cons of the various pending bills, they noted that the Arabs would view "Administration acceptance of any additional legislation on the Arab boycott as a shift in the Administration's position in response to the Israeli lobby."[32] The Commerce Department, Counsel's Office, and State Department supported the option to modify opposition to additional legislation by working with key Members of Congress for an amended bill. In so-called Option 1, the Treasury and Labor Departments and Cannon, Marsh, Friedersdorf, Scowcroft, and Seidman supported the following policy:

> Maintain the position outlined in your November 20 statement and strongly oppose all additional legislation as unnecessary and counter-productive, but do not indicate that you would necessarily veto any additional legislation thus leaving open the possibility of compromise later if sufficient opposition to the legislation does not develop.[33]

Although he was known for his "hands off" style, Ford took a direct interest in the issue and personally initialed his support for Option 1.

In spite of these concerted efforts by the Ford administration to satisfy domestic pressure groups, it was no surprise when the boycott issue became a point of debate between Ford and Carter in the 1976 election campaign. Seeing the political weaknesses of Ford's positions on the issue, Carter supported the anti-boycott campaign and chided Ford for his failure to comply with stricter legislative controls. In August, labor leader George Meany weighed in on the side of further legislation and White House polls of Congress indicated strong opposition to the administration's positions.[34] Interestingly, Meany took this position in spite of the fact that the jobs for many Americans, including union members, were directly tied to trade with the Arabs.

When anti-boycott legislation was appended to the Export Administration Act, Doc Morgan was again in the spotlight and warned that he could not "delay any longer."[35] The initial White House strategy was to get the Tax Conference to delay consideration of the Ribicoff tax penalty approach until after Labor Day in September or, failing that tactic, to further delay by referring the Export Act to the Joint Atomic Energy Committee under the guise of the nuclear provisions also contained within the bill.[36] The administration was keenly aware of "the foreign policy implications of active support [for legislation] and ... risks involved for non-opposition and quiet support insofar as foreign policy questions are concerned."[37] Although the administration publicly continued to maintain its opposition to any further boycott legislation, privately it considered a "stand-in position" of accepting "non-opposition to the modified Stevenson Amendment."[38]

While officials involved with foreign policy issues such as Kissinger advocated opposition to any anti-boycott legislation, those concerned with domestic policy and reelection supported some modified version of the proposed legislation with the Stevenson bill viewed as the least damaging. In short, White House advisers tried to minimize the negative political fallout by constructing a policy whereby Ford might be seen as taking a positive role. With this goal in mind, they suggested that possibly the President might compromise by publishing the names of firms on the current list of firms that might have complied with the boycott and that this might, at least temporarily, appease the Zionist and Jewish lobby.[39]

In the face of relentless political opposition, the Ford administration was forced to backtrack. On 4 October 1976, Ford ordered Morton to deliver the information regarding the boycott and specific U.S. businesses to Congress.[40] Press Secretary Nessen also announced that Ford had signed the Tax Reform Act,

> under a provision of which foreign source income attributable to certain boycott-related activity will lose the tax benefits of the foreign tax credit, the Domestic International Sales Corporations ("DISCs"), and the deferral of United States tax on foreign source income.
>
> These actions have put an end to foreign discrimination against American firms or citizens on the basis of religion, national origin, race, color, or sex. Public disclosure of boycott reports will further strengthen existing policy against the Arab boycott of Israel without jeopardizing our vital interests in the Middle East.[41]

Clearly, domestic political pressure had forced the Republican administration to retreat on its anti-boycott legislation stand and to bow to the anti-boycott campaign. However, the anti-boycott campaign continued to gather momentum and remained a volatile election issue. Sensing the political weakness of the Ford administration on the issue, Carter used his opposition to the Arab Boycott to political advantage. In what might be billed as "the concert of the two tenors," both Ford and Carter addressed the issue in speeches and the presidential debates. Although Carter was described as having "outdone himself on the boycott issue,"[42] Ford defended his record and was advised to respond to queries on the boycott in the following manner:

> ... let me give you a few facts on this matter. First, the so-called Arab boycott has been around for almost twenty-five years. I have opposed it since its inception ... All Presidents since 1952, Democrat and Republican alike, have opposed the boycott. But all Presidents ... have refrained from reckless promises ... on the issue.
>
> Five American Presidents have not done so because:
> – they knew the boycott was ineffective.
> – Second, because they knew that legislative efforts against the boycott would be enormously difficult to enforce, would needlessly embitter the Arabs; and would push them into more extreme and perhaps more effective economic sanctions against Israel.
>
> Let me return to Mr. Carter's position for a moment ... he has already threatened economic warfare against the Arab nations if they re-imposed an oil boycott. Now he is threatening them again. A candidate who does that as President will find it enormously difficult if he becomes President [again] to act as the honest broker bringing both sides together for a permanent peace.[43]

The Treasury Department added the following arguments:

> – The only way to end the boycott is to address its underlying causes ... they [sic] boycott is rooted in the conflict between Israel and the Arab countries, so that the surest means of ending it is to bring an end to the basic conflict.
> – The success of the Administration's diplomatic and economic efforts in the Middle East has come because the U.S. has followed an even-handed policy ...
> – Nor should we forget the role played by our major friends in the area. Iran supplies 60% of Israel's oil. Saudia Arabia [sic] has been a stalwart against connumism [sic] in the area. For the U.S. to declare economic warfare on

these nations – as Carter threatened – could cause enormous harm to the interests of both Israel and the United States.[44]

Although some would dispute the claims of U.S. objectivity regarding the Arab Israeli conflict, the arguments regarding the history and impact of the Arab Boycott are apt. Indeed, Ford's warnings to Carter proved prescient.

As president, Carter would find himself in the same role as his predecessor. Although Carter had used the anti-boycott campaign to his own political advantage, once in office he found the shoe was on the other foot. The campaign against the boycott continued to escalate, resulting in further legal actions. Now it was the turn of the Carter administration to "avoid an adverse effect on ... Middle East diplomacy and not disadvantage legitimate American business activities abroad."[45]

While the White House staff recognized that the conflict was essentially "between support for the anti-blacklist principle and the risks of hostile reaction and loss of business from the Arab world,"[46] some advisers, particularly White House liaisons and those close to the Jewish American community, argued that Carter should live up to campaign promises endorsing boycott legislation. They formed a chorus in support of anti-boycott legislation. Focusing on the contradictions between U.S. economic interests and domestic concerns, this chorus told the President that:

> You and your Administration are on record as supporting boycott legislation which would prohibit U.S. firms from complying with the Arab blacklist of other U.S. firms ... At bottom, this problem involves a conflict between support for the anti-blacklist principle and the risks of hostile reaction and loss of business from the Arab world. Particularly after your statements during the campaign, *we do not think your Administration can be less forthcoming on this issue than the Business Roundtable* [emphasis in original].[47]

Singing the same tune, some Jewish community leaders even rather disingenuously argued that the campaign was "an American issue" and that they were "not seeking anti-Arab legislation."[48]

In the end, a compromise was reached, not through the White House or Congress, but by direct meetings between a Round Table of key corporate businesses (including Exxon, General Electric, General Motors, among others) and major pro-Zionist organizations (Anti-Defamation League, the American Jewish Committee and the

American Jewish Congress). The resulting Round Table provided for limited modifications to proposed legislation and endorsed language that:

- prohibited religious or ethnic discrimination;
- prohibited U.S. firms from refusing to conduct business with a boycotted country as a condition of doing business in a third country;
- prohibited U.S. firms from enforcing foreign boycott;
- prohibited U.S. firms from responding to requests for boycott-related information and
- enabled both sides to declare a victory of sorts.

In May 1977 Carter endorsed the compromise along the following lines recommended by Eizenstat.

I am pleased to announce that an agreement has been reached by the Anti-Defamation League, the American Jewish Committee and the American Jewish Congress with the Business Roundtable on legislative language for the anti-foreign boycott bill presently being considered by the Senate, and that I can strongly recommend Congressional approval of that language ... In my view, one of the most gratifying aspects of the agreement is its reasonable balance between the need for stringent controls over the undesirable impact on Americans of foreign boycotts and the need to allow continuation of American business relations with countries engaging in such boycotts.[49]

However, the matter refused to die. With increased legislation, the anti-boycott supporters turned their attention to the control and regulation of the new laws. The Carter administration continued to grapple with these knotty issues well into 1978.

The Arab voices in this protracted opera were almost all heard only off-stage. The anti-boycott campaign was conducted in an atmosphere almost totally devoid of *any* information regarding the historical or legal purposes behind the boycott or the reasons for its continued existence. The Arab regimes, in particular Saudi Arabia, were keenly aware of the problems faced by U.S. businesses. In meetings with the Saudi Ambassador, Ali Abdullah Alireza, the boycott was referred to as a "most nettlesome issue."[50]

Even in the face of stricter U.S. regulations and public opposition to boycott, Arab nations did not cut off trade or business with the U.S. And indeed, Arab states showed a willingness to compromise to maintain economic ties, although some new business, particularly from Saudi Arabia, did go to Japan.[51] But in keeping with their preference for quiet, behind the scenes contacts with top officials or businessmen, neither the Saudis nor any other oil-rich Arab nations vigorously and publicly reacted to the anti-boycott campaign. None launched a massive media blitz to counter the pro-Zionist allegations against the boycott or to take the opportunity to educate the American public about the Palestinian cause and the reasons for the boycott. The lack of Arab response also may reflect the lack of consensus among Arab regimes, particularly the conservative monarchies and oil-rich regimes, over the boycott and its implementation.

Ironically, the strongest commentaries explaining the Arab position on the boycott did not come from Arab leaders but from U.S. officials. Strong statements against more stringent legislation came from William Simon, Secretary of the Treasury, coupled with equally strong support for Israel.[52] Former U.S. Ambassador to Egypt Richard Nolte, in a letter to the *New York Times*, and Secretary of State Cyrus R. Vance, in a statement before the International Finance Subcommittee of the Committee on Banking, Housing and Urban Affairs (1977), both addressed the issue, albeit largely from the perspective of U.S. interests. Amin Hilmy II, Permanent Observer to the United Nations, League of Arab States, also published a closely reasoned exposition of the boycott as "an instrument of Peaceful Self-Defense" in the *National Journal*.[53] However, these few statements had virtually no impact on either the general American public (most of whom never read or heard about them) or on political forces nationally or domestically.

The anti-boycott campaign afforded the Arabs a prime opportunity to educate the American public about the legal aspects of the boycott and its legitimacy under international law, but they failed to do so. They also failed to draw attention to the relationship of economics and human rights within the context of the struggle of the Palestinians for national rights of self determination. Finally, they missed the opportunity to draw public attention to the similarities between American boycotts against nations like Cuba or Korea and the Arab Boycott of Israel. Finally, they missed the opportunity to draw public attention to the similarities between American boycotts against nations like Cuba or Korea and the Arab Boycott of Israel. Nor did the PLO or groups in the U.S. sympathetic to the Palestinians call attention to the boycott as one means (admittedly unsuccessful) of redressing their grievances against Israel. The Arabs were largely invisible much like the ghost of Banquo at the banquet scene in Verdi's operatic version of *Macbeth*.

Nor were there any serious economic repercussions. Arabs, particularly oil-rich Arab regimes, continued to recycle their petro-dollars, buying U.S. merchandise, and investing in U.S. banks and firms. U.S.–Arab economic relations remained relatively robust – even cordial – over the next several decades even as U.S. support for Israel and military involvement in the region escalated. These economic ties continued with little opposition until the late 1990s, when in face of continued Palestinian resistance to the Israeli occupation of the West Bank, East Jerusalem, and the Gaza Strip, some Muslims and Arab Americans, and later Arab consumers, particularly students, rallied behind formal and informal boycotts of U.S. goods. Firms such as Burger King and Starbucks Coffee were singled out, forcing the closure of several outlets in the Arab world. But with the notable exception of Syria, these boycotts had little support for Arab governments. However, even these small grassroots movements infuriated Israel and the Zionist lobby. The ADL demanded the Commerce Department investigate the campaigns but were told nothing illegal had occurred.[54]

Economic boycotts have the potential to be effective in gaining political leverage and publicizing a cause, but Arabs and Arab Americans have thus far failed to make use of that potential. The state of Israel and its supporters clearly understand the potential of Arab economic clout which is precisely why they seek to monopolize the debate and upstage all other performers. During the 1970s campaign, pro-Israeli lobbies not only wrote the libretto, they sang the lead roles, formed the chorus, and largely conducted the entire campaign.

The anti-Arab Boycott campaign demonstrates how a fully articulated and embellished campaign, coupled with the severe vocal deficiency of the Arabs, resulted in changes to U.S. laws and policies, even in face of presidential opposition. The successful orchestration of the anti-boycott campaign ensured that the laws governing compliance against the boycott would survive over the long term. Operating within the system, the anti-boycott campaigners utilized all the available lobbying techniques on local, state, and national levels.

In so doing, they exhibited considerable political acumen as well as a sophisticated knowledge of the dynamics driving politics in the United States. In contrast, the Arab governments and Arab Americans failed to counter, let alone to adopt proactive strategies to bolster or to protect the Arab Boycott.

10

Act Two: The Carter Administration

Carter came to the presidency having campaigned on a pro-Israeli platform. In his earlier political career, Carter, a devout Christian, visited Israel where he expressed his deep sympathy for the Jewish state.[1] On a number of occasions, he had also publicly opposed the creation of a separate Palestinian state.[2] As previously described, Carter had jumped on the Zionist lobby's anti-Arab Boycott drive for stronger legislation governing compliance with the boycott. In spite of the traditional reluctance of Jewish voters to support candidates who seemed to mix religion (Christianity) with politics, Carter received 75 percent of the Jewish vote. In addition, over 60 percent of the major donors to the Democratic party were Jewish in the 1976 presidential election and although Carter was considered a "long shot," 35 percent of his funding came from Jewish donors.[3]

In the 1990s, many Jewish American organizations, following the Israeli far right Likud party line, changed the tune against mixing religion and politics and forged what is, in fact, an inherently contradictory alliance with the Christian right. The resulting duet between these disparate voices has managed thus far, with careful orchestration, to sing in harmony.

In addition to the perennial pressure by the Zionist lobby, Carter also had to face the mounting furor over rising oil prices and shortages. Although some have perceived Carter as caving into Arab, particularly Saudi, demands regarding oil producers,[4] there were strong voices within the White House against OPEC. Stuart Eizenstat and others blamed elements within OPEC for the price rises and sought to rally the American public against it. As Eizenstat explained, "the point was finding some way to rouse people's attention and focus it."[5] Not coincidentally, Eizenstat was a consistently strong and effective pro-Israeli voice in Washington.

There was also the key issue of arms sales to Arab governments. The arms sales to Saudi Arabia are an instructive example of the push-pull effect on foreign policy. Within the White House, liaisons with the Jewish community argued strenuously against arms sales to Saudi Arabia or any other Arab state;[6] others in the State Department and Pentagon favored sales. The White House and the Pentagon have historically encountered major difficulties in securing public or Congressional support for arms sales to Arab states. During the negotiations to secure Senate approval for sales of F-15s to Saudi Arabia, a Pentagon official reported that "We didn't do anything there that AIPAC didn't have within hours. Our briefing papers. We went to brief congressmen on the sale, and AIPAC already had rebuttals to our briefings." He attributed the leaks to "friends of Israel in the Pentagon."[7]

However, Saudi contacts with key Senators, especially Abraham Ribicoff, paid off when the Senate voted to approve the sale. A strongly pro-Israeli voice in the Senate, Ribicoff's visit to Saudi Arabia and Syria earlier in 1978 had caused him to reassess his previous hostility to these Arab states.[8] Following the Senate approval for the sale of F-15 fighter jets to Saudi Arabia in 1978, the Pentagon began to campaign for the sale of the new airborne warning and control system (AWACS). The Pentagon pushed for these sales because they helped to bolster the flagging American aircraft industry, furthered direct ties with the Saudi monarchy and helped to pay for research and development (R&D). The Pentagon took on the task of lobbying for the sales in Congress. The Saudis were asked only to make an appearance. A young, American-educated, prince duly made the Congressional rounds to counter media stereotypes, or in the words of one lobbyist, to "dehorn the monster."[9]

Because the sales could not go through until the after the 1980 elections, Carter, who was not opposed to the sales, asked that the incoming president, Ronald Reagan, be consulted. In an anecdote he often tells in lectures or question and answer periods, Prince Bandar, later the Saudi ambassador to the United States, went to see the President elect, Reagan, in California. Reagan asked only one question, "What is the Saudi position on the Soviet Union?" Bandar replied that it had always opposed it, even before the Cold War, because it was an atheist regime. After this short meeting, Reagan's office issued a statement in favor of the sales. Subsequently, even with the support of the Pentagon and the White House, Reagan still had to placate the Zionist lobby and Israel although Congressional approval was eventually forthcoming.[10]

Several factors assisted this lobbying effort. First and foremost, the Pentagon supported and lobbied for the sale. Oil companies also favored it and may have contacted Reagan to secure his support. Finally, the entire process took place within a short three-month period before pro-Israeli forces, that traditionally opposed arms sales to any Arab nation, had time to organize a major campaign in opposition. However, the Saudi regime found these exchanges so bruising that it turned to Great Britain for further purchases of armaments.

With this backdrop, Carter might have been expected to adopt pro-Israeli policies and to take stances that were generally hostile or unfavorable to the Arabs and the Palestinians in particular. However, several factors militated against the continuation of policies that completely rejected or ignored the legitimacy of Palestinian rights. In contrast to Ford and Reagan, Carter was very much a "hands-on" president. In his memoir, Hamilton Jordan, chief staff aide and perhaps Carter's closest adviser, emphasized that the best way to convince Carter on any given issue was to marshal arguments in writing.[11] He was open to debate and, in marked contrast to George W. Bush and his coterie, showed considerable flexibility and willingness to change previously held opinions. Carter received information and advice from numerous sources with indirect and direct contacts in the Arab world. In particular, William Quandt of the National Security Council (NSC) offered advice on the Arab Israeli conflict and the necessity of addressing Palestinian grievances. Quandt was on record as having called for an independent Palestinian state.

Once in office, the Carter administration, like Ford's and the first Bush administration, initiated a "reassessment" of policy regarding the Arab Israeli conflict. However in contrast to his predecessor, Carter was very much an active participant in this reassessment, eliciting and listening to a wide range of opinions. On the down side, Carter, an outsider to Washington politics, was sometimes criticized for not working more closely with Congress.[12] Carter hated small talk and never established warm or close relations with members of Congress. He refused to "do those necessary things to cement relationships that ultimately make things happen." [13] The openness of the Carter administration to new policy initiatives on the Arab Israeli conflict also raised the red warning flag to Israel and the Zionist lobby in the United States.

AIPAC immediately marshaled its considerable resources to lobby the White House and Congress against any consideration of a Palestinian homeland.[14] AIPAC and other Zionist organizations provided White House officials with a steady stream of anti-Palestinian and anti-PLO materials. After Carter publicly referred to Palestinian refugees as having been forced out of their homes in 1948, AIPAC head Morris Amitay protested that the president might not know the "actual facts" and sent him material from I.L. Kenen and the pro-Israeli *Facts and Myths, 1976* (published by AIPA almost every year).[15] The Anti-Defamation League (ADL) of B'nai B'rith and others also opposed contacts with the PLO or any hearing of the PLO case before the U.S. public.[16]

Some officials within the White House also acted as direct liaisons to communicate the opinions and policies of the Israeli government and Zionist lobby to Carter and other government officials. As the 1980 presidential campaign heated up, direct exchanges between the White House and the Zionist lobby increased. Alfred Moses was brought in as a special adviser to act as a conduit to the Jewish community. He clearly viewed the position as a way of not only improving communications between the Jewish community and Carter, but also as a means to influence foreign policy. Hamilton Jordan complained directly to the State Department that although Cyrus Vance, Secretary of State, viewed Moses' job as a "political assignment," Moses "views the job predominantly as a post for contributing special perspectives and insights into policy formation and then effectively communicating administration decisions back to gain support in a critical constituency group."[17]

The Palestinians could not hope to match such extensive ground-floor contacts or input into policy formation. This remains the case to the present day. Opposition to the Palestinians and the Arabs was even more pronounced in Congress, whose members consistently pressured Carter to maintain a solid pro-Israeli policy. Although he enjoyed a Democratic majority in Congress, Carter failed to mobilize or to sustain Congressional support for more flexible policies toward the Palestinians. One of the major failures of his presidency was Carter's inability or reluctance to orchestrate Congressional support for his policies.[18] Carter's failure to establish a working relationship with Congress, and to recognize its important role in "selling" and implementing policy, played into the hands of the more extreme Zionist lobbyists and their supporters on the Hill and damaged his effectiveness, not only on Middle East issues, but on a wide range of other policy initiatives as well.

In the face of heavy contravening pressures and precarious support from even the Democrats on the Hill, it is not surprising that Carter and his advisers sought to mollify supporters of Israel. To address Jewish concerns, Carter, Vice President Walter Mondale, Cyrus Vance and Zbigniew Brzezinski of the NSC held a high-level meeting with key Jewish leaders in July 1977. Brzezinski recommended that during this meeting the word "homeland" should be avoided as it had associations with the Balfour Declaration. He also argued that the term "defensible borders" should not be used because it implied the incorporation of most of the Occupied Territories, which the Arabs opposed.[19]

By this time, the administration had dropped Kissinger's step-by-step procedure, implemented during the Ford administration, instead espousing a comprehensive settlement reached through the Geneva Conference. While Kissinger saw the Arab Israeli conflict as only one piece of the global Cold War puzzle, Carter saw the problem as a regional one. The Carter administration accepted the fact that a comprehensive settlement necessitated a solution to Palestinian demands for self-determination.

When meeting with Carter, Jewish leaders emphatically voiced their concerns about the Geneva conference and a comprehensive settlement. They also opposed negotiating with the Palestinians, preferring agreements with individual Arab governments. Brzezinski explained that the administration hoped to achieve a comprehensive peace reinforced with security arrangements to forestall any Arab or Palestinian attempts to redraw the borders. Former Ambassador to the U.N. Arthur Goldberg retorted that only the United States could act as an intermediary and that all the parties involved had to accept Resolution 242. Goldberg concluded that the ambiguities in Resolution 242 were not accidental but purposeful. Goldberg certainly knew about the ambiguities of the resolution since he had largely been responsible for the drafting and acceptance of 242 after the 1967 war. Passed after the 1967 Arab Israeli War, Resolution 242 called for the establishment of permanent borders among the belligerent parties, withdrawal of Israeli forces from occupied territories and a just settlement of the refugee issue. It explicitly did not demand the return of all the territories occupied by Israel in 1967 or the creation of any sort of Palestinian state; indeed, the resolution did not even mention the Palestinians by name. Hence, from the Palestinian point of view, the Resolution failed to address the key sources of the conflict.

After listening to the concerns of the Jewish leaders, Carter voiced his own intentions. He emphasized his commitment to the security and continued existence of Israel. He stressed that, in his opinion, a separate Palestinian nation would be a threat to peace and that other Arab nations, namely Egypt, Jordan and Syria, were similarly concerned. He also emphasized that politically it would be easier for him to espouse the Israeli cause but that such an approach would not bring peace and that a more open approach was needed.[20]

Although not stated overtly at the July meeting, Carter's policy by the summer of 1977 may be summarized as follows: the assembly of the Geneva Conference, with the attendance of all parties, including some form of Palestinian representation; the return of most of the Occupied Territories to the respective Arab nations; some form of Palestinian autonomy, preferably in conjunction with Jordan; full peace agreements between the Arab nations and Israel; and the maintenance of a firm U.S. commitment to the security of Israel. The administration did not commit itself to any specific border realignments but definitely did not envisage an independent Palestinian state between Israel and Jordan. Nor did it have firm recommendations on the status of Jerusalem. But even this slight shift in policy was too much for the Zionist lobby.

Anwar Sadat's personal initiative and trip to Israel in 1977 undermined Carter's attempts to reconvene the Geneva conference. It also seriously damaged – perhaps destroyed – the possibility of a comprehensive settlement. In fact, Sadat was continuing the step-by-step, separate approach begun by Kissinger under Nixon, and continued under Ford.[21] By this time, it seems likely that Kissinger had sold Sadat on the personal, domestic and international benefits to be gleaned from his leadership of the step-by-step process and in signing a separate peace with Israel. His bold move also placed Sadat, who as a young man had wanted to be an actor, center stage. The Palestinians were thereby denied any visible role – acting only as an invisible force off-stage.

Although still publicly committed to a comprehensive settlement, the Carter administration supported Sadat's efforts, while maintaining back door contacts with the Palestinians. These contacts took several forms. From the outset of Carter's presidency, numerous and increasingly active Arab American groups had sought meetings with the president and top level officials. William Quandt generally favored such meetings, while Brzezinski, who wanted to keep foreign policy decisions within the purview of the NSC and Department of State, was reluctant to open up the consultative process. Representatives of the National Association of Arab Americans (NAAA) met with Midge Costanza, assistant for public liaison, and a representative from NSC in February but did not discuss the Palestinian issue.

As noted in Chapter 6 on Arab American lobby groups, it took considerable pressure from Arab American groups and sympathetic members of Congress for the White House seriously to consider a meeting with Arab Americans in late 1977. However, even as the Arab Americans gathered at the White House for the 11:45 meeting on 15 December, Carter was in the midst of a press conference announcing that, owing to its continued rejection of Resolution 242, the PLO had excluded itself from the peace process.

Although Carter's meeting with the Arab Americans lasted for about half an hour, the discussion involving the Palestinians was largely moot owing to the earlier public rejection of PLO participation in the peace process. It is virtually impossible to imagine that a president would make a similarly crucial statement on any matter of import to Israel, moments before meeting with Jewish Americans.

However, even as the process that included only Israel, Egypt and the United States moved haltingly toward Camp David, Carter kept private channels of communications open with the PLO. It is impossible to ascertain exactly how close the Carter administration came to direct negotiations, but meetings did continue. For example, George Ball and Landrum Bolling, president of the Lilly Endowment (a highly respected Indianapolis based philanthropic foundation established in 1937 by the Lilly family who had made a fortune in pharmaceuticals), briefed White House officials on meetings with Arab and Palestinian leaders. Writing that continued land seizures in the Occupied Territories were a major obstacle to peace, Bolling stressed that Israeli dissidents and doves (these were the supporters of the peace process as opposed to the more hardline, far right Israeli political parties) wanted a settlement with the Palestinians. Bolling also publicly affirmed the right of Palestinians to self-determination and advocated that Israel return to the 1967 borders.[22] Senators Findley and Abourezk also kept Carter informed of their exchanges with PLO leaders, including Yasir Arafat. Although Carter replied that only acceptance of Resolution 242 would "open the possibility of direct discussions,"[23] other members of his administration met with Palestinians. In Europe, Issam Sartawi, the PLO European Counselor who was subsequently assassinated, twice met with U.S. Ambassador Milton Wolf.[24]

However, the meeting between Zuhdi Terzi, the PLO representative to the U.N., and the U.S. Ambassador to the U.N., Andrew Young, caused a firestorm of protests fanned by the Zionist lobby and Young was forced to resign to prevent further political damage to the administration.[25] From within the White House, Ed Sanders, a leading proponent of the Zionist line, was an outspoken critic of

Young. Sanders went so far as to recommend that Carter tell the American people that his decision to accept Young's resignation "was not based on pressure from any country or any group of Americans. It was based on my determination that it was in the best interest of the United States …"[26] Unfortunately, but perhaps not coincidentally, the protests followed after a flurry of exchanges during which the PLO had agreed to accept Resolution 242 if it were stretched to include mention of Palestinian rights to self-determination. This potential breakthrough, strongly supported by Carter, failed when Israel, Egypt, Jordan and Syria rejected it. Because at this critical historic juncture the PLO enjoyed considerable international support, it missed an opportunity by not pushing harder for a reworking of the U.N. 242 formula to include mention of the Palestinians.

Why did exchanges between the U.S. and the PLO continue after Brzezinski had said "bye-bye PLO" and the Palestinians had been excluded from Camp David? Simply because, in spite of the pro-Zionist lobby forces both outside and within the White House, the Carter administration was still committed, in principle at least, to a comprehensive settlement. The problem was that the Camp David process was actually a continuation of the separate peace, step-by-step approach. As the 13 days at Camp David attest, the Carter administration worked hard to pave the road for an Arab Israeli peace treaty. The agreements reached at Camp David have been described as the product of Carter's perseverance and knowledge of the conflict "down to the last comma and period."[27] But, for the Palestinians, the Framework for Peace in the Middle East proved to be a dead-end road, as the Oslo Agreements also proved to be, over a decade later.

The framework failed to address directly Palestinian rights to self-determination, that is, an independent Palestinian state. It divided the Palestinians into several separate entities; it did not address the difficult issues of Jerusalem and the right of return of the Palestinians; and it attempted to impose a settlement without the participation of the PLO.[28]

Although Carter contended that the agreement provided for the implementation of Palestinian national rights, a close analysis of the agreement's exact wording belies that contention. As Carter himself noted, the term "autonomy" had multiple meanings, particularly for Israeli Prime Minister Menachem Begin, who at one juncture emphasized that "autonomy does not mean sovereignty."[29] After leaving office, Carter acknowledged that Begin probably would have rejected "the possibility of an independent Palestinian state."[30]

The building of new Israeli settlements in the Occupied Territories became one of the major points of contention among the relevant parties. The failure to deal directly and clearly with this vital issue was a major shortcoming of the agreement. Why Carter, knowing the crucial importance of this issue, failed to put the supposed agreement of settlements (no new settlements were to be constructed during the time talks leading to the implementation of the agreement were in process), is perplexing. It is probable that Carter and Sadat knew that Begin would refuse to sign an agreement calling for a freeze on new settlements. Pressing the issue might well have caused the negotiations to collapse. Carter and Sadat had both taken major political risks at Camp David and they needed an agreement. Subsequently, Carter admitted that the failure to address the settlement issue had been his biggest mistake in the negotiations.[31] The issue of the settlements remains a major obstacle to peace to the present day.

In fact, the administration had consistently ignored or chosen to misinterpret the political realities of the Arab world. Not only Arab leaders, but also high-ranking U.S. diplomats had warned that a separate peace or rejection of Palestinian self-determination was unacceptable to the Arabs. One career diplomat bluntly admonished Brzezinski over the "extraordinary misunderstanding about Arab attitudes toward the Palestinian state." He continued:

> ... the Saudi position was clear: it was that there could be no peace in the Middle East unless the rights of the Palestinians are recognized; that this includes the right of self-determination; and that everyone knows the Palestinians want a state of their own.
>
> ... The Arabs are convinced that there must be a state sooner or later or there will be no peace. In the interim a confederation with Jordan might work.[32]

The Carter administration chose not to heed this clear and realistic appraisal.

Even after the agreement for the Camp David Framework, Carter still had to exert extraordinary personal effort to secure a peace treaty.[33] To date, Carter, with the notable exception of Eisenhower, has been the only U.S. president willing to up-stage the Zionist lobby by putting his reputation and credibility on the line to achieve a peace settlement in the Middle East. Carter's March 1979 trip to the Middle East was a major political risk, taken against the recommendation of some of his top advisers. Long before the 1980 presidential election or Camp David, Senior Adviser Edward Sanders – a consistently pro-Israeli voice in the Carter White House – had recommended a low diplomatic profile. In a clear exposition of the anti-Palestinian and pro-Israeli position, Sanders wrote in 1978:

> If involvement in the Sadat–Begin peace process is too public, the Administration runs the risk of being blamed whenever difficulties arise ... We believe that a visible substantive American role is unnecessary ...
>
> The President has scored markedly at home by voicing explicit opposition to an independent Palestinian (any diminution of that position would be harmful). We believe that there would be no chance for peace today without Israeli strength and that continued maintenance of the Middle East military balance is essential to the smooth functioning of the peace process ... Needless to say, serious domestic problems could occur if assistance to Israel is curtailed.[34]

Actually, Sanders was echoing the Israeli line: the continuation of the status quo, Israeli control over the Occupied Territories, no concessions whatsoever to the Palestinians and the maintenance of Israeli military superiority over the entire Arab world. Sanders went so far as to recommend that Israeli settlements remain in Sinai for "perhaps ten years hence" and that the same formula be applied to the West Bank under a "Jordanian presence."[35]

In 1979, when Carter was supporting the aforementioned efforts to work out a new U.N. resolution including the PLO's formula to include mention of Palestinian rights to self-determination in Resolution 242, Sanders advocated dropping all efforts to secure a U.N. resolution, the veto of "any resolution in that forum" and a continuation of the autonomy talks as provided for in the Camp David framework.[36] These recommendations echoed the positions of the Zionist lobby, but were submitted, not by an outside pressure group, but by an "in-house" adviser. Subsequent administrations, particularly the George W. Bush White House, have had numerous top-level advisers who continually advocate a straight pro-Zionist foreign policy.

On the opposite side, Hamilton Jordan encouraged Carter to take the initiative; he thought a trip to see Sadat might well be the only way to secure a peace treaty. In an emotional appeal, Jordan wrote, "I just have a gnawing feeling now that the chance for peace is slipping away and that only you can save it."[37] Choosing to ignore the voice of the Zionist lobby, Carter followed Jordan's direction.

Carter personally visited Sadat and Begin in Egypt and Israel, placed his political career at risk and achieved a full peace treaty between the old antagonists.

Carter also managed to persuade Begin and Sadat to sign a joint letter promising to begin negotiations regarding the Occupied Territories within one month of ratification of the peace treaty. According to the text:

> The purpose of the negotiations shall be to agree, prior to the elections, on the modalities for establishing the elected self-governing authority (administrative council), define its powers and responsibilities, and agree upon other related issues ... [T]he objective of the negotiations is the establishment of the self-governing authority in the West Bank and Gaza in order to provide full autonomy to its inhabitants.[38]

Jordan was to be invited to join the negotiations and the delegations of Egypt and Jordan could include Palestinians, "as mutually agreed." In the event Jordan refused and Egypt and Israel would hold talks alone.

However, the treaty and attached agreements did not provide the means to secure Palestinian self-determination. If there were any doubts on the point, the remarks exchanged by the three leaders on the occasion of the signing of the treaty at the White House demonstrated that the resolution of the Palestinian demands was not central to the treaty. Carter never mentioned the Palestinians; Sadat side-stepped the issue and, as is perhaps superfluous to note, Begin ignored the Palestinians altogether. In effect, the Carter administration permitted Begin to trade Sinai for a peace settlement with Egypt, Israel's most potent military foe, and for continued control over Gaza, the West Bank and all of Jerusalem.

Yet Carter remained personally committed to a comprehensive settlement, including some form of autonomy for the Palestinians. His success at Camp David and in obtaining an Egyptian Israeli peace treaty earned him public accolades from politicians on the Hill. Only Senators Findley and Abourezk spoke out about these arrangements' shortcomings.[39] Had circumstances been different during his last year in office, Carter might have moved more forcefully on the Palestinian issue, but he was beset with domestic problems (inflation) and international crises (the Iranian revolution and the protracted problems over the American hostages).

During the election year, the White House monitored U.S. public opinion on a wide range of issues pertaining to the Middle East, particularly the Palestinians. Although polls indicated sustained support for Israel coupled with a moderate increase in sympathy for various Arab states, support for the Palestinians remained minuscule. In a 1979 Harris poll, respondents were asked to agree or disagree to the following proposition: "As the most powerful force among Palestinian Arabs, the PLO should be in on any negotiations about Gaza or the West Bank, even if the PLO are [sic] terrorists."[40]

Loaded as it was with value judgment and bias, the question elicited a predictable negative response. It is uncertain what the responses might have been if the poll had characterized the PLO appropriately as the "sole legitimate representative of the Palestinian people." Fifty-seven percent of the respondents disagreed with the statement, yet even under this wording, 34 percent still felt the PLO should be included. On the other hand, the same poll indicated that 61 percent thought the Palestinians should be included in the negotiations, while 65 percent thought the PLO should recognize Israel's right to exist before being recognized by the United States. However, polls indicated that Egypt's image had considerably improved and that Americans actually ranked it higher than Israel.[41] But given that the polls did not indicate widespread grassroots support for the Palestinians – as opposed to the well-established and vocal support for Israel – it was unlikely that Carter, an incumbent beleaguered with a host of problems, could launch a successful drive to include the PLO in negotiations. Carter also had to contend with the strong contrapuntal voices of the Zionist lobby both domestically and within his own administration.

Thus Carter's successes in the Middle East did not translate into voter support and he received a smaller percentage of the Jewish vote in 1980 than in 1976. Jody Powell, Press Secretary under Carter, opined years later that working toward a peace settlement had not gained Carter or any other president domestic political support because "if you're going to get an agreement, you're going to have to push the Israelis some too. If you do that, you're going to get a backlash in this country."[42] The alliance of the Christian right and Zionist lobby during the George W. Bush administration has created even bigger obstacles to an even-handed policy.

11
Curtain Calls: Present and Future

The effects of lobbyists and special interest groups on policy formation are complex and cannot be quantified. The previous chapters described the successes of Greek Americans on the Cyprus issue and Jewish Americans in securing support for Israel. Why did these groups succeed when others failed? Both these ethnic/religious special interest groups mobilized around one issue and used built-in cultural attitudes to gain public and political support for their causes. Greek American efforts to secure an arms embargo against Turkey, and Jewish American campaigns against the Arab Boycott, both pitted these special interest groups against the White House, State Department and the Pentagon. Although Greek Americans obtained Congressional support for an arms embargo on Turkey, their victory was relatively short lived. There are three main reasons for this failure. First, Turkey had the ability and political will to pressure the United States and to impinge upon its perceived strategic interests in maintaining U.S. military bases on Turkish soil. Second, Turkey's decision to close U.S. bases strengthened White House and Pentagon efforts to convince Congress to drop the embargo. Third, as the efforts of the Greek American lobby dwindled, some Greek American leaders were even persuaded to drop their active support for the embargo. Thus the Greek American success had only a short-term impact and did not result in any long-term changes to U.S. policies regarding Cyprus, Greece or Turkey.

In contrast, the Zionist lobby has remained committed to Israel over the long term. Jewish Americans continue to care about Israel and they have a single issue orientation that enjoys support from all levels of government from the White House and Congress down to city and state levels. Consequently, the influence of Jewish Americans far exceeds their proportion of the general population. The impact is magnified by small voter turn outs in elections across the country (the 2004 presidential election was a notable exception). Furthermore unless Americans are dying as a result of foreign entanglements as in Vietnam during the 1960s and 1970s or in Iraq in the contemporary era, the overwhelming majority of Americans remain apathetic to international events and do not demand to be involved in either the formation or implementation of foreign policy.

Consequently, a few passionately committed Zionists and Zionist organizations, who make major financial contributions to political parties and candidates and who turn out to vote, exert considerable political force and retain overwhelming support in Congress. These groups have successfully tapped into deeply embedded cultural values of the Judeo-Christian tradition, guilt over the Holocaust, and fears of being labeled anti-Semitic.

During the Cold War, pro-Zionist lobby groups reasoned that support for Israel was in the best interests of the United States in its struggle against the Soviet Union. From the 1950s on, the Israeli governments pursued cordial relations with nations along the periphery of the Middle East, particularly in Africa and Asia. Seeking formal political and military alliances with the United States, Israel persistently tried to convince Washington that it would be a useful surrogate for U.S. interests against the Soviet Union in these vital areas. Simultaneously, pro-Zionist pressure groups in the U.S. worked to persuade the White House that close ties with Israel had both geo-strategic and domestic political advantages. However, in spite of considerable Congressional and domestic pressure, presidents in this era managed to avoid most formal treaties with Israel. Successive administrations kept their options open by maintaining a precarious balance between economic and military aid for Israel and continued ties with dependent, conservative Arab regimes.[1]

On the other hand, Zionist lobbies and interest groups had considerably more success in securing firm, long-term commitments from both the House of Representatives and the Senate. The consistent, bipartisan support for Israel is evidence of that success. Congressional support for financial and political aid to Israel has been virtually assured for over 30 years. The continued, largely unquestioned allocation of billions of dollars in economic and military aid for Israel is a crucial example of the power of lobbies and domestic pressure groups. Although U.S. economic aid may be an essential life support system for Israel, no Arabs, not even Egyptians and least of all Palestinians, are dependent on U.S. assistance for national survival, nor is any of their aid assured of Congressional approval from year to year.

By 2004 the overwhelming pro-Zionist tilt in Congress resulted in the passage of a Global Anti-Semitism Review Act whereby the U.S. Department of State is required to monitor and combat anti-

Semitism throughout the entire world. With fulsome support from Zionist lobby and interest groups this act, that does not define anti-Semitism, easily passed through Congress. If enacted this act will have a further chilling effect on balanced debate on the Arab Israeli conflict and policy in the entire Middle East. It remains to be seen how Arab governments and Arab Americans will react or whether they will launch their own lobby campaigns to be included as "Semites" within the rubric of the new law.   .

Politicians on every governmental level must take the power of the Zionist lobby into account. Zionist lobbyists and interest groups have proven their ability to punish opponents by turning out voters, giving or withholding campaign monies, and supporting candidates who favor its agenda. The Zionist chorus drowns out other voices. By singing refrains with anti-Arab/Muslim stereotypes, the chorus plays to prevailing negative cultural attitudes. By repeating the same words and phrases over and over, Zionist supporters have successfully co-opted the rhetoric of debate; in other words, they "stay on message." They need no advice on effective lobby techniques and are consistently very skillful in formulating and waging effective campaigns to further their interpretation of Israeli interests.

The anti-Arab Boycott campaign is a prime example of the Zionist lobby's ability to attain long term, systemic changes through new legislation and implementation of new laws. In contrast to Turkish reactions to the Cyprus issue, oil rich Arab nations had the ability but lacked the political will and cohesion to make the U.S. pay for policy decisions detrimental to their interests. Nor did Arab Americans and their allies launch a campaign to counter Zionist arguments on the Arab Boycott. Thus in contrast to the case of Cyprus and Turkey, the White House has had little incentive to pressure Congress to oppose Zionist demands. Indeed, the White House has a good deal to lose, particularly on the domestic political front. As the case of the anti-Arab Boycott campaign demonstrates, lobbyists can have a decisive impact on Congressional legislation.

In addition, some Arab governments have found it convenient to focus on the power of the Zionist lobby to camouflage their own weaknesses and failures. These include their inability to secure a just settlement to the Arab Israeli conflict, their considerable shortcomings in providing basic human rights for all their citizens and their refusal to establish democratically elected systems. Similarly, U.S. policymakers have sometimes used the high visibility of the Zionist lobby as a cloak to cover U.S. economic, military and political aggressions in the Middle East.

U.S. support for authoritarian client regimes in the Arab world has historically placed Arab Americans, most of whom detest and oppose these regimes, at a distinct disadvantage in dealing with the White House and Congress. Arab Americans often find themselves in an adversarial position vis-à-vis the U.S. government, in marked contrast to the cordial relations enjoyed by Jewish Americans. The differences between the meetings of White House officials with Jewish Americans and those with Arab Americans demonstrate that Arab Americans would be well-advised to keep social exchanges to a minimum, to make two or three key points with recommendations for U.S. policy in a forceful, respectful fashion and to make these points repeatedly.

If they hope to compete on anything approaching even terms, pro-Arab groups would be wise to adopt long term, unified and vigorous agendas. To mount successful lobby campaigns, Arab American organizations need to expand and develop the trend toward unified efforts. ADC and other Arab American and Muslim organizations have had some success in countering stereotypes, particularly at the grassroots level, but even in this realm much remains to be done. Undoubtedly, the attacks of 11 September, the subsequent war in Afghanistan, the occupation of Iraq, Israeli attacks in the Occupied Territories and the concomitant increase of suicide bombings, have all exacerbated the problems faced by Arab American domestic pressure groups.

In some cases, campaigns could be coordinated with other like-minded ethnic and religious groups. To maximize impact, campaigns also need to be made in cooperation with efforts by Arab governments and/or the Arab League. Finally, Arab lobby efforts need to be directed toward the two major themes likely to resonate with U.S. voters and the general public: namely, economics and human rights. Both hold the potential of increasing the effectiveness of active Arab lobby campaigns and altering U.S. foreign policy.

In spite of pervasive negative stereotyping of Arabs and Muslims and vast ignorance or misconceptions about the history of the Arab Israeli conflict, the U.S. public still expresses considerable support for a negotiated settlement and the creation of some form of Palestinian state. Likewise, the public is generally hostile to massive foreign aid packages to any nation; hence in their publicity campaigns aimed for the general U.S. public, pro-Israeli lobby and interest groups tend to ignore or downplay the enormous amounts of money the U.S. government gives to Israel on an annual basis. Both sentiments have, however, yet to be translated into political will.

At this juncture, it should be emphasized that although the U.S. public is sympathetic to the human rights plight of Palestinians or other oppressed people, Washington may or may not act on those sentiments. The U.S. government's inaction, quiescence, or silence over the continued contravention of basic human rights in the Occupied Territories and elsewhere are instances in which predetermined foreign policies have taken precedence over the protection of human rights. Without laboring the point, it suffices to say that the United States has historically supported human rights on a selected, case-by-case basis.

As previously noted, public opinion in the United States is not generally the determining factor in forming foreign policy. Although lobbyists and special interest groups try to create a favorable climate of opinion for the acceptance of their goals, the U.S. public does not vote on matters of foreign policy. If Americans did vote on foreign policy, it is likely that Cyprus would be unified and the Palestinians would have an independent state of their own.

For a brief interval, the Carter administration attempted to redefine the terms of debate on the Arab Israeli conflict but ultimately settled for a continuation of the step-by-step process. Subsequent administrations, both Democratic and Republican, have continued that policy. The result has been a process described by William Quandt as an "overvaluation of the strategic relationship with Israel and the underinvestment in peacemaking."[2] The failures of Camp David and Oslo show that only a comprehensive settlement has any hope of success. No one should be thrown off track by the step-by-step approach that has allowed Israel and the U.S. to control the process. As a consequence, Israel has confiscated more land, built more settlements and maintained its military occupation over the Occupied Territories; it has also prevented the establishment of a viable Palestinian state.

Following September 2001, the Bush administration moved toward a full strategic alliance and acceptance of Israeli policies throughout the Middle East – something Israel and its supporters had wanted for many years. The Zionist lobby had successfully paved the way by preparing the U.S. public for such an alliance. Second, they helped to place Zionist supporters in key government roles. By 2003, over 50 years of concerted lobby and pressure group efforts had paid off, with Israel successfully convincing many in Washington that "my enemies are your enemies." Although many neo-conservatives viewed the alliance with Israel as in the best interests of the United States, others argued that this close alliance fails to serve the best interests of the United States, or in long run, that of Israel.

With their assured support from Congress, Israel and Zionist pressure groups in the U.S. need not fear attempts, even from the White House, to alter U.S. polices. As long as it has unqualified economic and political support in Congress, Israel has almost no incentive to modify its actions regarding settlements in the Occupied Territories or toward its treatment of the Palestinians. The ability of Zionist pressure groups to rally Congress behind fervent support for Israel caused the failure of both Ford and Carter's initiatives to secure compromises from all the parties to the conflict. As a result, rather than the president conducting the Congressional orchestra on matters of policy in the Middle East, Israel managed it from backstage.

Before any president can effectively advocate a comprehensive settlement, Congress's unquestioned support and willingness financially to underwrite Israel must be modified in the wider interests of the United States. The problems of U.S. relations in the Middle East far exceed the narrow script of ethnic or religious special interest groups. Although a resolution of the Arab Israeli conflict will not solve all of the region's problems, it would alleviate much of the hostility, anti-American feeling and violence that characterizes the area at present.

Notes

INTRODUCTION

1. For a fuller exposition of this point see: Ian Buruma, "How to Talk About Israel," *New York Times Magazine*, 31 August 2003.

I THE LIBRETTO: MAKING FOREIGN POLICY

1. A number of "insiders" as well as scholars have written about how foreign policy is made, while others have concentrated specifically on U.S. relations with Middle Eastern states. Among them are: George Kennan, *Around the Cragged Hill: A Personal and Political Philosophy* (New York: W.W. Norton & Company, 1993); Thomas E. Mann, ed., *A Question of Balance: The President, The Congress and Foreign Policy* (Washington, D.C.: The Brookings Institution, 1990); Eric Alterman, *Who Speaks for America? Why Democracy Matters in Foreign Policy* (Ithaca: Cornell University Press, 1999); Steven L. Spiegel. *The Other Arab-Israeli Conflict: Making America's Middle East Policy from Truman to Reagan* (Chicago: University of Chicago Press, 1985).
2. Zbigniew Brzezinski, Exit Interview, 20 February 1981, Jimmy Carter Library. Hereafter cited as JCL.
3. Kennan, *Around the Cragged Hill*, p. 189.
4. See: Kennan, *Around the Cragged Hill,* and Spiegal, *The Other Arab-Israeli Conflict,* for fuller interpretations of this process.
5. James A. Nathan and James K. Oliver, *Foreign Policy Making and the American Political System* (Boston: Little, Brown and Company, 1983), p. 69.
6. Minutes: National Security Council Meeting, 28 March 1975, Office of the Assistant to the President for National Security Affairs, Henry Kissinger and Brent Scowcroft, Temporary Parallel File, Box A5, Gerald Ford Library, Hereafter cited as GFL.
7. Hal Saunders to WWR (Walter "Walt" Rostow, National Security Adviser in Kennedy and Johnson administrations), Confidential "NODIS" Memo, 24 July 1968, LBJ/NSC, reel 7; Louis Harris and Associates Summary of Survey of Attitudes of Americans toward Arab Israel conflict, January 1975, Robert Goldwin, File: Jewish Organizations (1), Box 2, GFL.
8. Robert Goldwin to Donald Rumsfeld, 1 May 1975, Robert A. Goldwin, File: Jewish Organizations (1), Box 2, GFL.
9. Goldwin summary of survey, sent to Rumsfeld and others, May 1975, Robert A. Goldwin, File: Jewish Organizations (1), Box 2, GFL.
10. The most extensive scholarly study on public opinion and polls regarding the Middle East is: Eytan Gilboa, *American Public Opinion Toward Israel and the Arab-Israeli Conflict* (Lexington, MA: Lexington Books, 1987). Gilboa was with the Hebrew University of Jerusalem.

11. See: Hernando Calvo Ospina, *Bacardi: The Hidden War* (London: Pluto Press, 2002). Ospina traces the machinations of the Cuban lobby and, in particular, the role of the Bacardi firm in influencing and manipulating U.S. policy toward Cuba over the last four decades.

12. "How America Doesn't Vote," Editorial, *New York Times*, 15 February 2004.

13. Ibid.

14. Voting reform could backfire," Editorial, *International Herald Tribune*, 12 May 2004.

15. "Democrats fight for city's favor," *Detroit Free Press*, 23 October 2003.

16. Hugh B. Shannon, "Voters! The true political reformers," *Free Times* (Cleveland, Ohio), 15–21 March 2000. For further discussion on the minimal input of the public in foreign policy matters, see: Alterman, *Who Speaks for America?* Also: Interview with Abdeen Jabara, attorney and Arab-American community activist, 20 July 1994.

17. Kevin Phillips, *Arrogant Capital: Washington, Wall Street, and the Frustration of American Politics* (Boston: Little, Brown & Company, 1994).

18. Gerald R. Ford, *A Time to Heal* (New York: Harper & Row, 1979), p. 350.

19. Goldwin Papers, Box 2, GFL.

20. Hamilton Jordan Memo to President Carter, June 1977, Hamilton Jordan Confidential File, Box 34, File, "Foreign Policy/Domestic Politics Memo, HJ Memo, 6/77," JCL.

21. Ibid.

22. Mark Danner, "How the Foreign Policy Machine Broke Down," *New York Times Magazine*, 7 March 1993.

23. Jordan, Memo to President Carter, June 1977.

24. Ibid.

25. Ibid.

2 THE SCORE: MEDIA AND POPULAR CULTURE

1. Edward Said, *Orientalism* (New York: Pantheon Books, 1978); see also Said, *Covering Islam: How the Media and Experts Determine How to See the Rest of the World* (New York: Pantheon Books, 1981).

2. See among others: Michael Suleiman, *The Arabs in the Mind of America* (Brattleboro, Vermont: Amana Books, 1988); Jack G. Shaheen, *The TV Arab* (Bowling Green, Ohio: Bowling Green State University Popular Press, 1984) and *Reel Bad Arabs: How Hollywood Vilifies a People* (Northampton, MA: Interlink Publishing Group, Incorporated, 2001); Janice J. Terry, *Mistaken Identity: Arab Stereotypes in Popular Writing* (Washington, D.C.: American-Arab Affairs Council, 1985); Laurence Michalak, "Cruel and Unusual: Negative Images of Arabs in Popular American Culture," *ADC Issues*, January 1984; Edmund Ghareeb, ed., *Split Vision: The Portrayal of Arabs in the American Media* (Washington, D.C.: American-Arab Affairs Council, 1983). See also: Linda Steet, *Veils and Daggers: A Century of National Geographic's Representation of the Arab World* (Philadelphia: Temple University Press, 2000).

3. Norman Daniel, *Islam and the West: The Making of an Image* (Oxford: Oneworld, 1993). This is a revision of his earlier 1960 work.
4. Robert MacNeil, panel discussion at Columbia University, March 1993, cited in *Lies of Our Times*, June 1994. Pierre Salinger lecture, Coral Gables Congregational Church, 12 March 1996, Books on Books, C-Span, 2–3 June 1996 (lecture not published).
5. Noam Chomsky, *The Fateful Triangle: The United States, Israel and the Palestinians* (Boston: South End Press, 1983); David Croteau and William Hoynes, *By Invitation Only: How the Media Limit Political Debate* (Monroe, ME: Common Courage, 1994); Edward S. Herman and Noam Chomsky, *Manufacturing Consent: The Political Economy of the Mass Media* (New York: Pantheon, 1988).
6. James Fallows, *Breaking the News: How the Media Undermine American Democracy* (New York: Pantheon, 1996). See also: Nathan and Oliver, *Foreign Policy Making and the American Political System*. In *Republic of Denial: Press, Politics, and Public Life* (Yale and London: Yale University Press, 1999), Michael Janeway describes the radical changes in press coverage in the late twentieth century by referring to the "inertia of modern institutional life," p. 10.
7. In the United States, four mega giants (General Electric, Time Warner, Disney/Cap Cities, and Westinghouse) control a vast array of electronic and print news and entertainment sources. *The Nation*, 3 June 1996. James Aronson, *The Press and the Cold War* (New York: Monthly Review Press, 1970), p. 78. See Robert W. McChesney, *The Problem of the Media: U.S. Communication Politics in the 21st Century* (New York: Monthly Review Foundation, 2004) for an analysis of the media in the service of corporate profit.
8. Eric Alterman, *What Liberal Media? The Truth About Bias and the News* (New York: Basic Books/A Member of the Perseus Books Group, 2003).
9. Serge Halimi, "Myopic and cheapskate journalism," *Le Monde Diplomatique*, November 1998.
10. Martin Kettle, "If it's in the US, it's news, If not, forget it," *Guardian Weekly*, 16 May 1999, and Frank Rich, "The Weight of an Anchor," *New York Times Magazine*, 19 May 2002.
11. Louis W. Liebovich, "The Press as Presidential Antagonist," *National Forum*, Winter 2000.
12. Jeff Cohen and Norman Solomon, "Anti-Arab bigotry rampant in U.S. news," *Seattle Times*, 1 August 1992.
13. Samuel P. Huntington, *Clash of Civilizations and the Remaking of World Order* (New York: Simon & Schuster, 1996).
14. Glenn E. Perry, "Huntington and His Critics: the West and Islam," *Arab Studies Quarterly*, Vol. 24, No. 1, Winter 2002.
15. Patrick Seale, "Why is the West Afraid of the Arabs?" http://english.daralhayat.com/comment/01–2004/Article-20040130–63b7c417-c0a8–01ed-001c-22ffae711923/story.html, accessed 2 February 2004.
16. Joseph Kraft, "The Dark Side of Islam," *Washington Post*, 19 May 1981.
17. Terry Ahwal, "Media jump to conclusion: Muslims did it," *Detroit Free Press*, 30 April 1995.
18. "Terrorism hits home," *Detroit News*, 23 April 1995.

19. "Seeing Green: The Red Menace is Gone. But Here's Islam," *New York Times*, 21 January 1996.

20. "Terror Isn't Alone as a Threat to Mideast Peace," *New York Times*, 15 March 1996.

21. Kathleen Christison, "U.S. Discourse on Palestine: Perception vs. Reality," *Washington Report on Middle East Affairs*, April 2001, p. 25. See also Christison, *Perceptions of Palestine: Their Influence on U.S. Middle East Policy* (Berkeley: University of California Press, 1999). See also: Michael C. Hudson and Ronald A. Wolfe, eds., *The American Media and the Arabs* (Washington, D.C.: Center for Contemporary Arab Studies, Georgetown University, 1980) and *The Arab Image in the Western Media* (1979 International Press Seminar. London: Outline Books, 1980).

22. See studies by Suleiman, Shaheen, Michalak, and Terry; also see: Reeva S. Simon, *The Middle East in Crime Fiction: Mysteries, Spy Novels and Thrillers from 1916 to the 1980s* (New York: Lilian Barber Press, 1989). The latter has a useful annotated bibliography of the genre.

23. Edward N. Tivnan, *The Lobby: Jewish Political Power and American Foreign Policy* (New York: A Touchstone Book: Simon & Schuster, 1987).

24. For example see: Jonathon Wilson, "Operation Desert Hoops," *New York Times Book Review*, 14 April 1996, review of Zev Chafets, *Hang Time* (Warner Books Inc., 1996).

25. V.S. Naipaul, *Among the Believers: An Islamic Journey* (New York: Random House and Deutsche, 1981). See also: Naipaul, *Beyond Belief: Islamic Excursions Among the Converted Peoples* (New York: Random House, 1998). John Carey, "V S Naipaul among the Moslem zealots," *Sunday Times*, 4 October 1981.

26. John Marshall Papers, Rockefeller Archive Center, North Tarrytown, New York. Marshall served the Rockefeller Foundation in the Division of Humanities and Social Science from 1933 to 1970 and was the director of Villa Serbelloni (Rockefeller Foundation Bellagio Study and Conference Center) from 1959 to 1970. The book in question was: Ishak Musa Husaini, *The Moslem Brethren* (Beirut: Khayat's, 1956).

27. Joan Peters, *From Time Immemorial: The Origins of the Arab-Jewish Conflict* (New York: Harper & Row, 1984).

28. Albert Hourani, *Middle East Journal,* 1985; Norman Finkelstein, letter to the editor, *New York Times,* 26 December 1985; Edward W. Said, "Conspiracy of Praise," *The Nation,* 19 October 1985.

29. M. Petrovich, R. Roberts, C. Roberts, *World Cultures* (Morristown, NJ: Silver, Burdett, and Ginn, 1991), pp. 233, 608. Middle East Studies Association/Middle East Outreach Council, Text Evaluation Project (Ann Arbor, MI: Center for Middle Eastern and North African Studies, 1991) provides an extensive annotated review of texts available for use throughout the United States. Mohammad Arkoun in *Rethinking Islam*, trans. Robert D. Lee (Boulder, CO.: Westview Press, 1994; Paris: Jacques Grancher, 1989), refers to the "cultural poverty of the brief chapters devoted to Islam" in texts for both European and American students. See also: Letitia Creamean, "Membership of Foreigners: Algerians in France," *Arab Studies Quarterly*, Winter 1996. See also: William J. Griswold, *The Image of the Middle East in Secondary School Textbooks* (New York: Middle

East Studies Association, 1975) and Michael W. Suleiman, *American Images of Middle East Peoples: Impact on the High School* (New York: Middle East Studies Association, 1977).

30. Winthrop D. Jordan, Miriam Greenblatt, John S. Bowes, *The Americans: A History* (Evanston, IL: McDougal & Littell & Co., 1992), pp. 587, 914, 958.

31. Samuel P. Huntington, "The Clash of Civilizations?" *Foreign Affairs*, Summer 1993.

32. "The Islamic Cauldron," *Foreign Affairs*, May/June 1995. R. Emmett Tyrrell, Jr., "Chimera in the Middle East," *Harper's*, November 1976; J.B. Kelly, "Let's Not Leave It to the Arabs," *The Spectator*, 16 March 1991.

3 THE STAGE SET: IMAGES AND ATTITUDES

1. Ellen K. Coughlin, "Breaking the Prejudice Habit," *Chronicle of Higher Education*, 27 October 1995.

2. Robert D. Kaplan, "Tales From the Bazaar," *Atlantic Monthly*, August 1992; *The Arabists: The Romance of an American Elite* (New York: The Free Press, 1993).

3. Department of State, *United States Foreign Policy: An Overview*, January 1976, p. 29.

4. James E. Akins to Zbigniew Brzezinski, 24 September 1979, White House Central File (WHCF), CO-8, JCL.

5. Robert W. Komer to Ralph Dungan, 9 April 1964. Copy to George MacBundy. Lyndon B. Johnson National Security Files, the Middle East: National Security Files, 1963–1969. Microfilm edition, reel 8. Hereafter cited as LBJ/NSC. A White House aide to President Johnson, Komer was an Under Secretary of Defense for Policy.

6. William R. Polk Memo on U.S. Policy Toward the UAR to Walter Rostow, 7 April 1964, LBJ/NSC, reel 8. Polk was a recipient of Rockefeller Foundation fellowships and a staff member of the Middle Eastern Studies Center and Assistant Professor of Near Eastern Languages and History at Harvard before moving to the State Department.

7. Ibid.

8. As one example, see the long and extremely factual biography prepared for the state visit of the French leader Valéry Giscard d'Estaing, 17–22 May 1976. Ron Nessen Files, Box 28, or biographic sketches on U.S. diplomats, Ron Nessen Files, Box 41, GFL. Nessen was Press Secretary to President Ford.

9. See: CIA biographies on Israeli Prime Minister Levi Eshkol, 31 August 1967, or Ya'acov Herzog, Director General of the Israeli Prime Minister's office, 3 November 1966. LBJ/NSC, reel 7.

10. Fact Sheet, 5 June 1974, Charles McCall Papers, Box 31, GFL. McCall was Director of Research in the Ford White House.

11. Biographic Sketches, Saudi Arabia, 1977, WHCF, Co-52, JCL.

12. Biographic Sketches, Saudi Arabia, 1978, Staff Offices – Press (Advance) Office File, Box 9, JCL.

13. Anwar Sadat, Biographical Sketch distributed prior to his 1977 State Visit, WHCF, Box CO-24, JCL.
14. Interview with Richard Moe, Miller Center Interview Project, Carter Presidency Project, Vol. XII, 15–16 January 1982, p. 126, JCL. Moe was Chief of Staff to Vice President Walter Mondale.
15. Memorandum of conversation, 26 February 1968. Participants were: Rabin, Rostow, Israeli Minister Evron, General Amit and Harold H. Saunders. A State Department official, Saunders also served as an Assistant Secretary of State during the Carter administration. LBJ/NCS, reel 7.
16. Ibid.
17. LBJ/NSC, reels 7–8; see also, State Department background notes on Israel, 1974, circulated in advance of Yitzhak Rabin's visit, 10 September 1974, CO71, GFL.
18. Stuart Eizenstat, "American Jews and Israel in the Bush era," address given at Susan and David Wilstein Institute of Jewish Policy Studies, Los Angeles, 6 June 1989, Vertical File, JCL.
19. Ron Nessen Papers, Box 28, GFL.
20. Menachim Begin biography 1979, WHCF, CO-7, JCL. Reports on both Israeli and Arab leaders by NSC officials, notably William Quandt in the Carter White House, are more balanced and detailed. See biographies in WHCF, CO-40, JCL.
21. Al Moses Papers, Box 2, JCL. Moses, Special Adviser to Carter, acted as the White House liaison with the American Jewish community.
22. George W. Ball and Douglas B. Ball, *The Passionate Attachment: America's Involvement with Israel, 1947 to the Present* (New York: W.W. Norton & Co., 1992), p. 86.
23. Interview with Richard Moe, JCL.
24. Jack Watson Interview, Miller Center Interview Project, 17–18 April 1981, pp. 104–5, JCL. Jack Watson was Cabinet Secretary and Assistant for Intergovernment Affairs; he became Chief of Staff when Hamilton Jordan left to coordinate Carter's reelection campaign.
25. Seymour M. Hersh, "The Grey Zone: How a secret Pentagon program came to Abu Ghraib," *New Yorker*, 24 May 2004; see also: David Rieff, "Blueprint for a Mess," *New York Times Magazine*, 2 November 2003.
26. Susan Sontag, "Regarding the torture of Others: Notes on what has been done – and why – to prisoners, by Americans," *New York Times Magazine*, 23 May 2004.
27. Steven L. Spiegel, *The Other Arab-Israeli Conflict: Making America's Middle East Policy from Truman to Reagan* (Chicago: University of Chicago Press, 1985), p. 394.

4 PRODUCTION ASPECTS: LOBBY TECHNIQUES AND FINANCES

1. David E. Rosenbaum, "In a Test of Lobbying Muscle, Realtors Prevail," *New York Times*, 13 July 2003.
2. Jeffrey H. Birnbaum, *The Lobbyists: How Influence Peddlers Get Their Way in Washington* (New York: Times Books, 1992), p. 13. The dynamics of the lobbying process and the work of individual lobbyists and organizations

are detailed in a number of studies, including: Bruce C. Wolpe. *Lobbying Congress: How the System Works* (5th ed.) (Washington, D.C.: Congressional Quarterly, 1987).

3. As this study attests, the documentation from the Ford and Carter Presidential libraries supports these conclusions.

4. "Lobbyist's Sway Rises With G.O.P." *New York Times*, 3 April 2002.

5. Anne Wexler, Exit Interview, 12 December 1980, JCL.

6. Birnbaum, *The Lobbyists*, p. 235.

7. Joan Peters, "Report on Middle East Refugees," Marked "Not for Publication," 1977. Stuart Eizenstat Files, Box 235, JCL.

8. Hamilton Jordan, Box 37, JCL.

9. Gerald Rafshoon, Oral History Project, Miller Center Interview, 8 April 1983, JCL. Rafshoon handled Carter's public relations from his early career as a gubernatorial candidate in Georgia and then served as Assistant to the President for Communications.

10. Stuart Eizenstat speech at Temple Sinai, Washington, D.C., 22 February 1991, Vertical File, JCL.

11. Stuart Eizenstat, Exit Interview, 10 January 1981, JCL.

12. CO70–71, Box 26, GFL.

13. Staff Offices, Jody Powell, Press Secretary, Box 82, JCL; see also: Vice Presidential papers, Box 17, CO 158, Box 50–52; CO 146, CO 71, Box 27, and David Lissy Files, Box 41; Co 159 in GFL for representative samples of this type of letter and White House records on pressure group campaigns. David Lissy was Associate Director, Domestic Council, and the political liaison with Jewish organizations in the Ford White House.

14. David Greenberg in *Nixon's Shadow: The History of an Image* (New York: W.W. Norton, 2004) describes Nixon's use of "spin" and his creation of different media images during his long, "checkered" political career.

15. Hamilton Jordan, *Crisis: The Last Year of the Carter Presidency* (New York: Putnam, 1982). Lloyd Cutler, Counsel to the President, Oral History Project, Miller Center Interview, 23 October 1982, JCL.

16. See: Fred H. Lawson in "The Truman Administration and the Palestinians," America and the Palestinians Special Issue, *Arab Studies Quarterly*, Vol. 12, Nos. 1 & 2, Winter/Spring 1990, for a detailed overview of the interrelationship of politics, domestic pressure groups and foreign policy during the Truman era.

17. The Electronic Daily Diary, Max Fisher, GFL.

18. Scowcroft Memo, 2 July 1976, CO 71, GFL.

19. Hamilton Jordan Memo to Warren Christopher, 8 April 1980, Hugh Carter's Files, Office of Administration, Box 37, JCL.

20. NSC Memo, 8 November 1974, CO70–71, Box 26, GFL.

21. CO 70–71, Box 26, GFL.

22. For documentation on the major Jewish American organizations and their relationships with Israel see: Lee O'Brien, *American Jewish Organizations & Israel* (Washington, D.C.: Institute for Palestine Studies, 1971, 2nd printing 1986); Ernest Stock, *Partners & Pursestrings: A History of the United Jewish Appeal* (New York: University Press of American, 1987); Edward N. Tivnan, *The Lobby: Jewish Political Power and American Foreign Policy* (New York: A Touchstone Book: Simon & Schuster, 1987).

23. Joyce R. Starr, *Kissing through Glass: The Invisible Shield between Americans and Israelis* (Lincolnwood, IL: NTC/Contemporary Publishing Company, 1991). Starr was the White House liaison on Soviet Jews and Press Coordinator in the Jewish Community Affairs Division for Carter.

24. George W. Ball and Douglas B. Ball, *The Passionate Attachment: America's Involvement with Israel, 1947 to the present* (New York: W.W. Norton & Company, 1992), p. 86.

25. Max L. Friedersdorf (Assistant to the President for Legislative Affairs) Files, Box 6; Myron Kuropas Files, GFL. These files include extensive materials on the interrelationship between the White House and ethnic communities.

26. Joseph Pika in "The White House Office of Congressional Relations: Exploring Institutionalization," University of Wisconsin, 1979, and "Dealing with the People Divided: The White House Office of Public Liaison," paper prepared for delivery at the 1982 Annual Meeting of the Midwest Political Science Association, GFL, in which Pika discusses the creation and evolution of these offices.

27. Paul Findley, *They Dare to Speak Out: People and Institutions Confront Israel's Lobby* (Westport, CT: Lawrence Hill, 1985).

28. Mark Danner, "How the Foreign Policy Machine Broke Down," *New York Times Magazine*, 7 March 1993.

29. Lloyd Cutler, Exit Interview, JCL. Cutler was Counsel to the President.

30. Jimmy Carter, Oral History Project, Miller Center Interview, 29 November 1982, JCL.

31. Philipp Blom, *To Have and to Hold: An Intimate History of Collectors and Collecting* (Woodstock: The Overlook Press, 2003), p. 193.

32. Michael J. Malbin, ed., *Parties, Interest Groups and Campaign Finance Laws*, a conference sponsored by the American Enterprise Institute for Public Policy Research (Washington, D.C.: American Enterprise Institute for Public Policy Research, 1980).

33. Jim Drinkard, "With new law, GOP routs Democrats in fundraising," *USA Today*, 21 August 2003.

34. Ibid.

35. Ann Chih Lin and Amaney Jamal, "Navigating a New World: the Political Assimilation of Arab Immigrants," paper delivered at the Annual Meeting of the American Political Science Association, Washington, D.C.: 28–31 August 1997.

5 AN OVERTURE: THE CASE OF CYPRUS

1. Monteagle Stearns, *Entangled Allies: U.S. Policy Toward Greece, Turkey and Cyprus* (New York: Council on Foreign Relations Press, 1992). Not surprisingly, both sides underestimated the human costs to their opponents while exaggerating their own.

2. Laurence Halley provides a sympathetic account of the Greek side of the dispute in *Ancient Affections, Ethnic Groups and Foreign Policy* (New York: Praeger, 1985) while Paul Watanabe in *Ethnic Groups, Congress, and American Foreign Policy: The Politics of the Turkish Arms Embargo* (Westport,

CT: Greenwood Press, 1984), gives the Turkish point of view. Watanabe is highly critical of the ethnic Greek lobby campaign against Ford's pro-Turkish policies. See also: Suha Bolukbasi, "The Cyprus Dispute and the United Nations: Peaceful Non-Settlement Between 1954 and 1996," *International Journal of Middle East Studies*, August 1998, pp. 411–34.

3. Watanabe, *Ethnic Groups*, pp. 107–11.

4. Gerald R. Ford, *A Time to Heal: The Autobiography of Gerald R. Ford* (New York: Harper & Row, 1979), p. 138.

5. Memo: Tom C. Korologos to Larry Eagleburger on Prominent Greeks, 29 August 1974, WHCF, CO 55 Greece, 8/9/74–4/30/75, GFL.

6. Max Kuropas, Box 7; Al Haig – Name File: file: Brent Scowcroft, Box 2; WHCF: McCrary name file ("Tex" John Reagan McCrary) of the Hellenic-American Institute, GFL.

7. Veto to The House of Representatives, 17 October 1974, WHCF, SP 2–3–14 and SP 2–3–15, Box 8, GFL.

8. Signing Statement, Ron Nessen Papers, Turkey 8/9/74–7/8/75, Box 125, GFL.

9. Comments from Members contacted for their reaction to the announced Turkish takeover of United States and NATO installations, n.d. [circa May–June 1975], Max Friedersdorf, Box 16, GFL.

10. Ibid., John Roussselot (R-Cal.).

11. Jack Calkins Memorandum to Robert T. Hartmann, 8 October 1975, Folder, Peter Agris, Hellenic Chronicle of Boston, Ron Nessen Papers, Box 51, GFL. Ford's meeting with Agris was characterized in an Evans–Novak column as so effective that Agris asked Greek leaders to support the president's position in favor of lifting the embargo. When the news became public, Agris's credibility among Greek Americans suffered and he even threatened to sue the journalists who released the information.

12. Charles Bartlett, "Vote on Turkey shows undisciplined Congress," *Washington Star*, 28 July 1975.

13. Statement by Congressman Morgan after meeting with Ford at the White House, 9 July 1975, Ron Nessen Papers, Box 125, GFL.

14. Statement by the President, n.d. given but date is 25 or 26 July 1975, Ron Nessen Papers, Box 125, GFL.

15. Robert J. McCloskey [Assistant Secretary of State] Memorandum for Honorable John Marsh, The White House, 24 September 1975, WHCF, CO 156, Turkey, Box 49, GFL.

16. Congressman Cederberg in GOP Leadership Meeting with the president, 24 September 1975, Robert Wolthuis, Box 2, GFL.

17. Statement by the president, 8 October 1975, Ron Nessen Papers, Box 125, GFL.

18. Jimmy Carter, *Keeping Faith: Memoirs of a President* (Toronto: Bantam Books, 1982), pp. 51, 458, 563.

19. Ford, *A Time to Heal*, pp. 137, 199, 244, 285, 288.

20. Department of State for Zbigniew Brzezinski, 22 April 1977, ND-44, JCL.

21. Dom Bonafede, "Presidential Focus, Turkish Arms Vote Discourages Staff," *National Journal Reports*, 2 August 1975.

6 THE CAST: PRO-ARAB LOBBYISTS AND INTEREST GROUPS

1. This discussion is based largely on interviews with diplomats, officials, and lobbyists for Arab governments conducted from 1994 to 2002. Although most preferred to speak off the record, these professionals generously provided detailed histories of Arab diplomatic efforts in the U.S. Any conclusions or errors in this rendition are solely those of the author.

2. Mohamed Heikal, *The Return of the Ayatollah* (London: Andre Deutsch, 1981), pp. 95, 158–9; Michael Ledeen and William Lewis, *Debacle: The American Failure in Iran* (New York: Alfred A. Knopf, 1980), p. 75.

3. Edward Said Interview with *Palestine Report*, 29 August 2001, Prlist@palestinereport.org accessed 29 September 2003.

4. Michael Suleiman, "The Arab Information Effort in North America: An Assessment," *Arab Studies Quarterly*, Vol. 8, Summer 1986; Nabeel A. Khoury, "The Arab Lobby: Problems and Prospects," *The Middle East Journal*, Summer 1987.

5. Suleiman, "The Arab Information Effort in North America."

6. Michael W. Suleiman, "The Arab Information Effort in North America – An Assessment," Zionist information and Arab Requisites for its Confrontation Seminar (ALECSO), 18 May 1985, Tunis, Tunisia, p. 5. In this paper, Suleiman estimated that in 1983 Maksoud gave 55 speeches, 22 press conferences, issued 43 communiques and participated in 13 conferences.

7. William Fulbright speech, "Old Myths and New Realities – the Middle East," 24 August 1970, U.S. *Congressional Record*, Senate, 14035.

8. Paul Findley letter to Jimmy Carter, 8 June 1979, WHCF – CO35–74, JCL; see also Paul Findley name file, JCL. Paul Findley, *They Dare to Speak out: People and Institutions Confront Israel's Lobby* (Westport, CT: Lawrence Hill, 1985).

9. Findley, *They Dare to Speak Out.*

10. See James A. Bill, *George Ball: Behind the Scenes in U.S. Foreign Policy* (New Haven: Yale University Press, 1997) for a definitive study of Ball's long and illustrious career in public service.

11. Statement of Intent in *Washington Report on Middle East Affairs*, November 2003, p. 5.

12. Named after the late Joseph Malone, a history professor at the American University of Beirut and a mentor for a number of academics in the field of Middle East studies.

13. Actionalert@saudi-american-forum.org.

14. www.irmep.org/irmep.htm, accessed 1 August 2004.

15. *Palestine Human Rights Bulletin*, Special Issue (Number 11), October 1978.

16. Graham E. Fuller, "Political Islam and U.S. Policy," *Middle East Affairs Journal*, Vol. 5, Nos. 1–2, Winter/Spring 1999; Ayad al-Qazzaz, "The Arab Lobby: Toward an Arab-American Political Identity," *Al Jadid*, 3:14, January 1997.

17. Stuart Eizenstat, Exit Interview, 10 January 1981, JCL.

18. Helen Samhan and Samia El-Badry are both experts on Arab American demographics. "The New Arab Profilers," *Arab American Business*, January 2003.
19. United States Census 2000.
20. Curt Guyette, "Shifting Sands," *Metrotimes* (Detroit), 16–22 June 2004.
21. Sami Khatib, "Financial Accountability and Responsibility in Arab-American Organizations," *Al-Hewar*, March 1993.
22. Janice J. Terry, "Community and Political Activism Among Arab Americans in Detroit," in Michael W. Suleiman, ed., *Arabs in America: Building a New Future* (Philadelphia: Temple University Press, 1999; reprinted in Arabic by Center for Arab Unity Studies).
23. James Zoghby, "Alarm Bells in America as Arab Americans Face Increased Demonization," *Al-Ahram Weekly*, 24 May 2000.
24. Intern Perspectives: *2001 Intern Summer Times*, ADC, Summer 2001.
25. Memo on NAAA, meeting 26 June 1975, ND18/CO1–7; Nessen Papers, Box 121, GFL.
26. Public Liaison: Midge Costanza, List of National Ethnic Groups, Box 88, JCL.
27. *AAUG Newsletter*, December 1977. Attendees included: Dr. Fouad Moughrabi, President-Elect and Abdeen Jabara, one of the founders of the organization and a human rights lawyer.
28. DPS Staff, Eizenstat, Box 235; WHCF – National Security, Defense, Box ND-39; WHCF, Box CO3 (CO 1(Arabs) 1/20/77–1/20/81), JCL.
29. William B. Quandt and Gary Sick Memorandum to Zbigniew Brzezinski, 26 August 1977, ND, Box 39, ND16/CO1–7, JCL.
30. Brzezinski Note, 30 August 1977, ND, Box 39, ND16/CO1–7, JCL.
31. Brzenzinski Memorandum to Hamilton Jordan, 2 September 1977, WHCF, Name File, AAUG/NAAA/Association, American, JCL.
32. Brzezinski Memorandum for the President, n.d., through Hamilton Jordan, ibid., and Tim Kraft.
33. Janice J. Terry, "The Carter Administration and the Palestinians," in Michael W. Suleiman, ed., *U.S. Policy on Palestine from Wilson to Clinton* (Normal, IL.: Association of Arab-American University Graduates, 1995).
34. The description of this meeting is based on: 30 May 1989 telephone interview with Dr. Michael Suleiman, former president of the Association of Arab American University Graduates (AAUG), and a member of the delegation that met with President Carter; *AAUG Newsletter*, December 1977; *The Voice* (NAAA newsletter), January 1978.
35. Staff Secretary, 12/15/77 File, Box 64; Staff Office, Speech Writers Chronological File, Box 12; WHCF, NS-Defense, ND-39, Box 39, JCL. These files contain notice of the meeting and a list of attendees, but no presidential talking notes, minutes, or summaries about the meeting.
36. Presidential Daily Diary, PD-21, Box 21, JCL.
37. *The Washington Report on Middle East Affairs*, April/May 1997.
38. Janice J. Terry, *The Role of Lobbies in the Formation of U.S. Policy in the Middle East* (Beirut: Center for Arab Unity Studies, 2002) (in Arabic); Christopher Madison, "Arab-American Lobby Fights Rearguard Battle to Influence U.S. Mideast Policy," *National Journal*, 31 August 1985.

39. James Zogby statement at Arab American Institute annual leadership conference. Lynette Clemetson, "Arab-Americans Gain a Higher Political Profile," *New York Times*, 19 October 2003.
40. *2004 Voter Guide to the Democratic Presidential Candidates*, Washington, D.C., Arab American Institute, 2003.
41. Niraj Warikoo, "FBI revokes its service award from Arab leader," *Detroit Free Press*, 9 October 2003; Brian Dickerson column, "Award flap is a credibility loss for FBI," *Detroit Free Press*, 13 October 2003.

7 THE CAST: JEWISH AMERICANS AND PRO-ZIONIST LOBBIES

1. Gabriel Sheffer, ed., *Dynamics of Dependence: U.S.-Israeli Relations* (Boulder, CO: Westview Press, 1987); Nimrod Novik, *The United States and Israel: Domestic Determinants of a Changing U.S. Commitment* (Boulder, CO: Westview Press, 1986). Novik, a foreign policy adviser to Shimon Peres, wrote this study under the auspices of the Jaffee Center for Strategic Studies. For further analysis, see Abraham Ben-Zvi (also of the Jaffee Center), *The United States and Israel: The Limits of the Special Relationship* (New York: Columbia University Press, 1993). Tony Smith, *Foreign Attachments: the Power of Ethnic Groups in the Making of American Foreign Policy* (Cambridge, MA: Harvard University Press, 2000) traces the involvement of a number of different ethnic groups including Jewish Americans. For a classic study on U.S. public opinion see: Eytan Gilboa (Hebrew University of Jerusalem), *American Public Opinion toward Israel and the Arab-Israeli Conflict* (Lexington, MA: Lexington Books, 1987).
2. For example: "Policy Background: The Essence of Israel's Mideast Policy: From Cease-Fire to peace" (Washington, D.C.: Embassy of Israel, 11 April 1969); "PLO Undermining the Cessation-of-Hostilities" (Washington, D.C.: Embassy of Israel, 15 February 1982).
3. For details on the major Jewish American organizations and their ties with Israel see: Lee O'Brien, *American Jewish Organizations and Israel* (Washington, D.C.: Institute for Palestine Studies, 1971, 2nd printing 1986) and Ernest Stock, *Partners & Pursestrings: A History of the United Jewish Appeal* (Lanham, MD: University Press of American, 1986).
4. Rachel Zoll, "More U.S. Jews in poverty, study says," *Detroit Free Press*, 11 September 2003.
5. National Jewish Population Survey 2000/2001, partially released in 2002; Lenni Brenner, "My People are American. My Time is Today," 24 October 2003, www.counterpunch.org/brenner10242003, accessed 24 October 2003.
6. Lenni Brenner, "My People are American."
7. "U.S. Jews don't share Shamir's views, poll finds," *Detroit Free Press*, 21 November 1991.
8. Zoll, "More U.S. Jews in poverty."
9. Evelyn Shuckburgh, *Descent to Suez: Foreign Office Diaries 1951–1956* (New York: W.W. Norton & Company, 1986), p. 254.
10. Brian Whitaker, "US Think Tanks Give Lessons in Foreign Policy," *Guardian*, 19 August 2002.

11. Joel Beinin, "Money, Media and Policy Consensus: The Washington Institute for Near East Policy," *Middle East Report*, No. 180, January/February 1993.

12. In *Kissing through Glass: The Invisible Shield between Americans and Israelis* (Lincolnwood, IL: NTC/Contemporary Publishing Company, 1991), Joyce Starr talks openly about these connections; her career is indicative of the process. Starr was the White House liaison on Soviet Jews and Press Coordinator in the Jewish Community Affairs Division for the Carter administration. Subsequently, she served on George Bush's Middle East campaign task force.

13. I.L. Kenen, *Israel's Defense Line: Her Friends and Foes in Washington* (Buffalo, N.Y.: Prometheus Books, 1981).

14. Richard B. Strauss, "The revolution in Washington's Middle East Policy," *Manchester Guardian Weekly*, 4 May 1986.

15. "The Washington Lobby," *Congressional Quarterly*, 5th ed.; Edward N. Tivnan. *The Lobby: Jewish Political Power and American Foreign Policy* (New York: Simon and Schuster, 1987) and Benny Burner, *The Lobby*, film 2002.

16. Robert I. Friedman, "The Anti-Defamation League is Spying on You," *Village Voice*, 11 May 1993. This provides a detailed account of ADL espionage activities and the allegations against it.

17. "Summary of Relevant Facts," ADC et al., V. ADL et al., Executive Summary, 21 October 1993.

18. John J. Fialka and Brooks Jackson, "Pro-Israel Lobby," *Wall Street Journal*, 26 February 1985.

19. Robert I. Friedman, "PACmen," *The Nation*, 6 June 1987.

20. David K. Shipler and Robert Pear, "Pro-Israel lobby turns its political mystique into clout," *Detroit Free Press*, 12 July 1987.

21. Hamilton Jordan Confidential File, Box 34, "Foreign Policy/Domestic Politics Memo, HJ Memo, 6/77," JCL.

22. Senate Assessment on Middle East, Work Plan, Foreign Policy Issues, 25 June 1977, Hamilton Jordan, Box 34, JCL.

23. http://www.cov.com/lawyers/seizenstat/biography.html, accessed 22 January 2004.

24. Stuart Eizenstat, "Stick with Kyoto: A Sound Start on Global Warming," *Foreign Affairs*, May/June 1998.

25. "American Jews and Israel in the Bush Era," Eizenstat address at Susan and David Wilstein Institute of Policy Studies, Los Angeles, 6 June 1989, Vertical File; Eizenstat Exit Interview, 10 January 1981, JCL.

26. Charles Kirbo [Kirbo, an attorney, was a close friend and valued adviser to Carter], Oral History Project, Miller Center Interview, 5 January 1983; Israel(74) WHCF, Foreign Affairs, Box FO-30; Edward Sanders Memorandum to Hamilton Jordan,17 February 1979 Edward Sanders, Staff Offices 1/15/79–6/18/79, Box I, JCL.

27. Eizenstat speech, 6 June 1989, Eizenstat File, JCL.

28. Ibid.

29. Stuart Eizenstat, *Moment,* January/February 1988, Stuart Eizenstat File, JCL.

30. For example see notes on 1 August 1977 Roundtable discussion between Jewish Community Representatives and Agency Officials, Public Liaison, Midge Costanza, Box 20, Box, 52, Box 55, JCL.

31. Alfred Moses letter to Jerold C. Hoffberger, 6 June 1980, Special Adviser to the President, A. Moses, Box 7, JCL. Hoffberger had been the owner of the major league baseball team, the Baltimore Orioles, a chair of the United Jewish Appeal (UJA) and a major contributor to the Democratic party.

32. David Aaron Memorandum for Stu Eizenstat, 9 January 1979, WHCF – CO35; CO-74, JCL.

33. Reports and notes on White House meetings with Jewish American groups, David H. Lissy (Associate Director-Domestic Council, Ford White House) Files, Boxes 38–43, GFL. For an example of a less cordial meeting see: "Notes on Meeting with Jewish Leaders," 6 July 1977, Stuart Eizenstat Files, Box 235, WHCF, ND16/CO 1–7, JCL. At the time, Jewish leaders, reiterating Israeli fears, opposed a comprehensive settlement that might force them to make concessions. Although he emphasized that he thought an independent Palestinian state would be a threat to peace, Carter forcefully argued that, although it would be easier for him politically to espouse the Israeli line, a balanced and more open approach was required.

34. Arthur Hertzberg, "The Illusion of Jewish Unity," in *Beyond Occupation: American Jewish, Christian, and Palestinian Voices for Peace*, Rosemary Radford Ruether and Marc H. Ellis, eds. (Boston: Beacon Press, 1990).

35. Jay D. Shulman and Susan L. Wiley, "PAC Contributions by the American Dental Association: Do Dollars Follow Policy Positions?" paper presented at annual meeting of the Southern Political Science Association, Atlanta, Georgia, 3–6 November 1994. Shulman and Wiley give a useful overview of the dynamics and political goals of a domestic interest group (dentists) in backing candidates that will hopefully support legislature favorable to the dental industry.

36. For a fuller account of this process see: Leopold Yehuda Laufer, "U.S. Aid to Israel," *Dynamics of Dependence: U.S.–Israeli Relations*, Gabriel Sheffer, ed. (Boulder, CO: Westview Press 1987).

37. As Haim Saban, a media magnate and major American supporter of Israel, emphasized in a rare interview, "I'm a one-issue guy and my issue is Israel." Andrew Ross Sorkin, "Schlepping to Moguldom: An Unlikely Hollywood Titan finds a new power base," *New York Times*, 5 September 2004. Known for his contributions to the Democratic party and friendship with President Clinton, Saban pledged $13 million to establish the Saban Center for Middle East Policy at the Brookings Institute in 2002.

38. *New York Times*, 5 September 2004, p. 4, and Fialka and Jackson, "Pro-Israeli Lobby."

39. "Price of Politics," *Arab American Business*, April/May 2004.

40. Ibid., p. 6.

41. Alexander, "Pro-Israeli PACs," p. 16.

42. "Foreign Aid: Under Siege in the Budget Wars," *New York Times*, 30 April 1995.

43. Laufer, "U.S. Aid to Israel," p. 139.

44. Tom Hundley, "Cash buys allies, influence for U.S.," *Detroit Free Press*, 25 November 1984.
45. World Development Indicators database, World Bank, July 2003.
46. Charles Mitchell, "Your $14 Billion at Work Abroad," *Detroit Free Press*, 24 July 1994; "U.S. Assistance to the State of Israel: The Uncensored Draft Report," Staff of the U.S. General Accounting Office, 24 June 1983. Mohamed El-Khawas and Samir Abed-Rabbo, *American Aid to Israel: Nature and Impact* (Brattleboro, VT: Amana Books, 1984) present a highly critical account of the aid program while A.F.K. Organski, *The $36 Billion Bargain: Strategy and Politics in U.S. Assistance to Israel* (New York: Columbia University Press, 1990) argues that the aid program is in the best interests of the United States and is not given as a result of lobbying pressures.
47. Thomas R. Stauffer, "The Costs to American Taxpayers of the Israeli-Palestinian Conflict: $3 Trillion," *Washington Report on Middle East Affairs*, June 2003; see also White House memos regarding changing rules to make Israel eligible for A.I.D. Development Loans, 1974, M. Friedersdorf, File: Middle East, Box 14, GFL.

8 ACT ONE: THE FORD ADMINISTRATION

1. Robert Goldwin Papers, Box 3; ND18/CO1–7. Goldwin was a Special Consultant to the White House. Meeting with Senator William J. Fulbright, 2 July 1975, Brent Scowcroft Files, Box 1, GFL.
2. Robert Goldwin Papers, Box 3, Memo on Ford meeting with Kristol, 15 November 1974,GFL.
3. Letter, Eugene Rustow to Ford, 21 April 1975, ND18/CO1–7, GFL.
4. Gerald Ford, *A Time to Heal: The Autobiography of Gerald R. Ford* (New York: Harper & Row, 1979), p. 286; CO71; CO159. The records for most of these meetings, especially when Kissinger was present, remain classified.
5. Lowell Cauffiel, "Window on the World," *Detroit Monthly*, October 1988, p. 73.
6. ND18/CO1–7; CO71; Box 27; Goldwin, Box 2; Lissy, Box 40, GFL.
7. Al Haig papers, Box 1, Len Garment Memo to Dave Parker, 28 August 1974. Al Haig was Assistant to the President.
8. Brent Scowcroft Memo, 2 July 1976, CO71, Box 27. Scowcroft was Assistant for National Security Affairs, GFL.
9. Ibid.
10. Ford, *A Time to Heal*, p. 247.
11. Richard Cheney Papers, Box 9, Middle East File, GFL. Cheney was Assistant to the President.
12. CO158, Box 50–52; CO146; CO71, Box 27, GFL.
13. David Lissy Files, Box 41; CO159, GFL. David Lissy was Associate Director, Domestic Council, and the political liaison with Jewish organizations.
14. David Lissy Files, Box 41; Ron Nessen Papers, PLO File, Box 124; CO1–7, GFL.
15. Richard Cheney meeting with president, notes on meeting, Brent Scowcroft, 17 June 1976, Cheney, Box 9, GFL.

16. Ron Nessen Files, Press Statement, 21 June 1976, Box 14, GFL; Beirut Evacuation Postponement, 19 July 1976, Ron Nessen Files, Lebanon, Box 123, GFL.
17. US Policy towards the PLO, Briefing Book 1976 election, 14 October 1976, William Baroody Papers, Box 3, GFL.
18. ND18/CO1–7, GFL.
19. Abraham Ben-Zvi, *The United States and Israel: The Limits of the Special Relationship* (New York: Columbia University Press, 1993), p. 99.
20. Max L. Friedersdorf Papers, Box 14, Middle East File. Friedersdorf was Assistant to the President for Legislative Affairs, GFL.
21. Ibid.
22. See Richard Curtiss, "Too Often Promised Land – American Public Opinion and the Arab–Israeli Dispute 1973–1980." 22 Session: Executive Seminar in National and International Affairs, Department of State, 1975–80.
23. Meeting with Eugene V. Rostow, 17 April 1975, talking points by Henry A. Kissinger to Ford, p. 3, Brent Scowcroft, Box 3, GFL.
24. Minutes, National Security Council Meeting, 28 March 1975, Office of the Assistant to the President for National Security Affairs, Henry Kissinger and Brent Scowcroft, Files (1972) 1974–77, Folder: NSC Meeting, Box A5, GFL.
25. CO159, GFL.
26. Ron Nessen Files, Box 28, File 3; Press Information for Sadat visit, October 1975.
27. Memorandum of Conversation (Ford, Kissinger, Scowcroft), 17 October 1975 in the Oval Office, Henry Kissinger and Brent Scowcroft Files (1972) 1974–77, Temporary Parallel File, Folder: Scowcroft memcons, 17 October 1975, Office of the Assistant to the President for National Security Affairs, Box A6, GFL.
28. Charles McCall Papers, Box 29, GFL. McCall was Director of Research.
29. Vern Loen Report, Memo to Brent Scowcroft through John O. Marsh, September 1975, Loen and Leppert, Box 23, GFL.
30. Ibid.
31. Meeting with the Senate Wednesday Club, 3 September 1975, Friedersdorf, Box 8, GFL.
32. See: Harold H. Saunders and Cecilia Albin, *Sinai II: The Politics of International Mediation* (Washington, D.C.: The Pew Charitable Trusts, 1991), for full text of agreement and discussion of its diplomatic evolution. Also see: "Early Warning System in Sinai," Report, No. 94–415, 94th Congress, 1975; "Early Warning System in Sinai," hearings before the Committee on Foreign Relations, United States Senate, 94th Congress, First Session on Memoranda of Agreements between the Governments of Israel and the United States, 6–7 October 1975, Washington, D.C.: U.S. Government Printing Office, 1975.
33. Conversation with Wayne Hays, in memo, Charles Lepport to Jack Marsh, 13 August 1975, Loen and Lepport, Box 23, GFL.
34. Max Fisher congratulations on Second Sinai Agreement, 3 September 1975, Wolthuis, Box 4; CO71, Israel, 1/1/76–1/20/77, WHCF, GFL.
35. FO3–2/CO157–164, GFL.
36. Brent Scowcroft, Bipartisan Leadership Meeting, Cabinet Room with president, 25 September 1975, Wolthuis, Box 2, GFL.

37. Henry A. Kissinger Memorandum for the president, 10 October 1975, Fulbright Speech on the Middle East, Brent Scowcroft, Box 1, GFL.
38. Q & A for the president concerning the statement by General George Brown, 14 November 1974, Robert Goldwin Papers, Box 2, GFL.
39. Henry Kissinger, GOP Leadership Meeting, 4 November 1975, Congressional Leadership Meetings, GOP, 11/4/75, Wolthuis, Box 2, GFL.
40. Memo on conversation, Congressional Bipartisan Leadership Meeting, 24 June 1976, Wolthuis, Box 2, GFL.
41. Ibid.
42. Stephen M. Bauer, *At Ease in the White House* (New York: Birch Lane Press books, Carol Publishing Group, 1991). Bauer was Presidential Social aide under Nixon, Ford and Carter. He clearly preferred the grander styles of Nixon and Ford to Carter's common folks touch.
43. William Baroody Papers, Box 8; Jeffrey P. Eves Papers. Eves was Director of White House Conferences 1974–76, GFL.
44. News Release, President Ford Committee, President Ford Committee Records, Box F37, GFL.
45. Letter, George Klein to Max Fisher, 28 June 1976, President Ford Committee Records 1975–6, Box F36, GFL.
46. Letter, Max Fisher to Richard B. Cheney, 2 August 1976, President Ford Committee Records 1975–6, Box F36, GFL.

9 A MAJOR PRODUCTION: THE ARAB BOYCOTT CAMPAIGN

1. Paul Lewis on boycott, *National Journal*, 19 June 1976.
2. Ibid.
3. Barbara Greene Kilberg Memo on Arab Boycott, 8 August 1975, Robert A. Goldwin Papers, Box 1, GFL. Kilberg was Associate Counsel to the President; following extensive research on the Arab Boycott, she made recommendations for presidential action.
4. David V. Pritchett, Office of Financial Resources, 17 February 1976, Seidman, Box 313, 28 February–1 March 1976, GFL.
5. Lewis, *National Journal*, 19 June 1976.
6. Background Paper: Arab Boycott Issues, Israel, 1–3 March 1976 (3); marked 'Limited office use', Seidman, Box 313, GFL.
7. Aaron J. Sarna, *Boycott and Blacklist: A History of Arab Economic Warfare Against Israel* (Totowa, N.J.: Rowman & Littlefield, 1987). Sarna's densely written account details the application of the boycott and the campaign against it from a pro-Israeli viewpoint. He also provides a chronology of steps taken against the boycott from 1975 through 1976. R.W. MacDonald in *The League of Arab States* (Princeton: Princeton University Press, 1965) describes the early Arab involvement with the boycott.
8. Statement by Sidney Sober, Acting Assistant Secretary for Near Eastern and South Asian Affairs, before the Subcomittee [sic] on International Trade and Commerce, House Foreign Affairs Committee, 13 March 1975. Ron Nessen Papers, Box 121, GFL. Nessen was told that he could refer to this testimony in question and answer sessions with the press.

9. Representatives Joshua Eilbert (PA), 12 March 1975; Fish (NY), 14 March 1975; Drinan (MASS), 23 September 1975, *Congressional Record.*

10. For a summary of these testimonies see Lewis, *National Journal*, 19 June 1976.

11. Sober statement, Ron Nessen Papers, Box 121, GFL.

12. Ibid.

13. Memo for the President, September 1975, David Lissy Files, Box 39, GFL. Lissy was Associate Director-Domestic Counsel and Ford's political liaison with Jewish organizations.

14. Kilberg Memo, 8 August 1975. Robert A. Goldwin Papers, Box 1, GFL.

15. Ibid.

16. Ibid.

17. Kilberg Memo, 5 September 1975, Robert A. Goldwin Papers, Box 1, GFL.

18. See: Goldwin, Box 1; Lissy, Box 39, Friedersdorf, Box 10, CO70, 71; Ron Nessen Papers, Box 121; Vernon Loen and Charles Leppert Papers, Box 1. Loen and Leppert were Deputy Assistants for Legislative Affairs (House); Robert Wolthius Papers, Box 3; Wolthius was Special Assistant to the President. See also: Papers of Counsel to the President, Edward C. Schmults, Boxes 7–8, and Vern Loen and Charles Leppert, Box 1, WHCF; Trade Boycotts, Box 3, GFL.

19. Sarna, *Boycott and Blacklist*, p. 95.

20. Kilberg Memo, 8 August 1975, Robert A. Goldwin Papers, Box 1, GFL.

21. Ibid.

22. Ibid.

23. Statement by the President, 20 November 1975, Ron Nessen Files, Box 1, GFL. Presidential decisions regarding the boycott legislation and enforcement in James E. Connor Memo to Philip Buchen, 3 November 1975. Marked 'Administratively Confidential'. President Hardwriting File, Trade-Arab Boycott (1), Box 45, GFL. For a full summary of these measures see Sarna, *Boycott and Blacklist*, pp. 93–5.

24. Background paper/Arab Boycott Issues, Seidman, Box 313, Israel, 1–3 March, 1976(3), GFL.

25. ADL Press Release, 28 November 1975, Robert A. Goldwin Papers, Box 1, GFL.

26. Boycott Background Paper, p. 4, Seidman, Box 313, GFL.

27. Cabinet Meeting Minutes, 6 January 1976, handwritten notes, John G. Carlson (Office of Press Secretary), Box 1 and James E. Connor, Box 5, File: 1976/01/07 Cabinet Meetings: Presidential Handwriting File – States Folder, Arab Boycott (2), Trade, Box 45, GFL.

28. Ibid.

29. Memo, no date, "Arab Boycott," Ron Nessen Papers, Box 121, GFL.

30. E.P.B. Discussion Paper: Administration Position on Arab Boycott Legislation, 28 April 1976, Seidman, Box 32, E.P.B. Memoranda, 24–30, 1976, GFL.

31. David Lissy Memo to Jim Connor, 5 April 1976, Presidential Handwriting File; Folder: Trade-Arab Boycott, Box 45.

32. Brent Scowcroft and L. William Seidman memo for the President, 6 May 1976, Presidential Handwriting File; Folder: Trade-Arab Boycott, Box 45, GFL.

33. Ibid.

34. George Meany, 25 August 1976, statement urging the Senate to pass the bill inhibiting U.S. businessmen from trading with the Arabs owing to the boycott. Ron Nessen Files, Box 1; Friedersdorf, Box 10, GFL.

35. Bob Wolthius Memorandum to Max Friedersdorf, 30 August 1976, Friedersdorf, Box 10, GFL.

36. Ibid.

37. Jack Marsh Memorandum for the President, 15 September 1976, Presidential Harndwriting File-States, Box 45, Folder: Trade-Arab Boycott (2), GFL.

38. Ibid.

39. David Lissy Memo on Boycott, 30 March 1976; Schmults, Arab Boycott, Box 8; Ron Nessen Files, Box 9, GFL.

40. Ron Nessen Files, Box 1, GFL. As noted, Morton had been found in contempt of Congress by a Subcommittee and was therefore forced to reveal the information.

41. Statement from the White House, 4 October 1976, Ron Nessen Files, Box 1, GFL.

42. Stef Halper Memorandum for Dave Gergen and Fred Slight, 20 October 1976, Dave Gergen Files, Box 1, GFL.

43. Ibid.

44. Ibid.

45. Zbigniew Brzezinski Memo to Rich Hutcheson, 7 February 1977, TA-4, Tal/Col (Arabs), JCL.

46. Bob Lipshutz, Stu Eizenstat, Bob Ginsburg Memo to the President, 12 March 1977, Robert Lipshutz Papers, Box 2, WHCF, JCL. As previously noted, Stuart Eizenstat, Assistant to the President for Domestic Affairs, had close ties with pro-Zionist groups and, although not directly involved in foreign policy, he paid close attention to Middle East issues.

47. Ibid.

48. Joyce Starr Memo to Robert Lipshutz and Stuart Eizenstat, 10 March 1977, Robert Lipshutz Papers, Box 2, WHCF, JCL.

49. Stu Eizenstat Memo to the President, 2 May 1977, DPS, Eizenstat Papers, Box 146; David Rubenstein Memo to Stu Eizenstat, 5 January 1978, WHCF, Eizenstat Papers, Box 143, JCL.

50. Notes on the Vice President's meeting with Saudi Arabian Ambassador, Ali Abdullah Alireza, 19 January 1976, CO128. Notes in the Nessen Files also refer to Saudi Arabia's awareness of the problem. Ron Nessen Papers, Box 124, Saudi Arabia File, GFL.

51. Boycott Background paper, Seidman, Box 313, GFL.

52. William Simon Statement in *National Journal*, 31 July 1976; Nolte wrote a letter to the *New York Times* and Vance spoke before the International Finance Subcommittee on the Committee on Banking, Housing and Urban Affairs, 1977.

53. Amin Hilmy II, *National Journal*, 31 July 1976 and *The Arab Boycott: Whys and Wherefores* (New York: Americans for Middle East Understanding, Inc. n.d. [probably 1976/77]).

54. The grassroots boycott movements in the Arab world and U.S. are described in fuller detail in: "Widespread Recognition of Growing

Arab-American Clout," *ADC Times*, October–November 1999; "Boycott with a difference," *Middle East International*, 31 May 2002; Richard H. Curtiss, "Arab Boycotts, Both Formal and Informal, Well Under Way," *Washington Report on Middle East Affairs*, November 2002.

10 ACT TWO: THE CARTER ADMINISTRATION

1. Portions of this chapter have been published in "The Carter Administration and the Palestinians," *Arab Studies Quarterly*, Vol. 12, Nos. 1 & 2, Winter/ Spring 1990 and "The Carter Administration and the Palestinians," *U.S. Policy on Palestine from Wilson to Clinton*, Michael W. Suleiman, ed. (Normal, IL.: Association of Arab-American University Graduates, Inc., 1995).

2. Edward "Ed" Sanders (Carter's Adviser for Jewish Affairs, 1978–80) Files, 8/10/79–3/4/80, Staff Office, JCL. Sanders obviously gathered these statements together to convince the Zionist lobby of Carter's pro-Israeli stance during the 1980 election.

3. 1977 Report on Jewish Vote, Hamilton Jordan's Files, n.a., Box 35, JCL. The report may have come from the Office for Domestic Affairs or from a special adviser on ethnic and domestic affairs.

4. Steven Spiegel, *The Other Arab Israeli Conflict: Making America's Middle East Policy from Truman to Reagan* (Chicago: University of Chicago Press, 1985), p. 317.

5. Stuart Eizenstat, Exit Interview, 10 January 1981, JCL.

6. Edward Sanders and Roger Lewis to Robert J. Lipshutz and Hamilton Jordan, 11 January 1978, Counsel's Office, Box 2, "Arab Boycott"; Edward Sanders to the president and vice president, 6 March 1978, Hamilton Jordan, Box 49, JCL.

7. David K. Shipler and Robert Pear, "Pro-Israel lobby turns its political mystique into clout," *Detroit Free Press*, 12 July 1987.

8. Richard H. Curtiss, "Too Often Promised Land – American Public Opinion and the Arab–Israeli Dispute 1973–1980" (22 Session: Executive Seminar in National and International Affairs, Department of State, 1979–80).

9. This account is based largely on off-the-record interviews, including a lengthy interview with one of the key paid lobbyists for Saudi Arabia.

10. William B. Quandt, *Peace Process: Diplomacy and the Arab–Israeli Conflict since 1967* (Washington, D.C.: The Brookings Institution, 1993).

11. Hamilton Jordan, *Crisis* (New York: Putnam's 1982), p. 42.

12. Frank Moore (White House, Congressional Liaison), Exit Interview, 17 December 1980; NS Oral History Project, Miller Center Interview, 18–19 September 1981; Richard Moe, Oral History Project, Miller Center Interview, 15–16 January 1982; James Fallows (speech writer), Exit Interview, 14 November 1978. Others alleged that Carter's puritanical style set him apart from the hard drinking and partying of some political and media figures. Jody Powell, Oral History Project, Miller Center Interview, 17–18 December 1981 and Lloyd Cutler, Oral History Project, Miller Center Interview, 23 October 1982, JCL.

13. Richard Moe (Mondale's Chief of Staff), Oral History Project, Miller Center Interview, 15–16 January 1982, JCL.
14. Telegram, Morris Amitay (head of AIPAC) to Jimmy Carter, 6 June 1977, Hamilton Jordan's Files, Box 34, JCL. See also telegrams and letters in Box ND CO-42, WHCF, and Palestine Liberation Organization Name File.
15. Letter, Morris Amitay to Hamilton Jordan, 17 August 1977, Office of Communications, Gerald Rafshoon Collection, Box 4, JCL.
16. See for example, ADL letters opposing a visa for PLO spokesperson Shafik al-Hout in 1979, Anti-Defamation League File, Name File, JCL.
17. Hamilton Jordan memo to Warren Christopher, 8 April 1980, Hugh Carter's Files, Box 37, Office of Administration, JCL.
18. Tip [Thomas] P. O'Neill Jr. with Gary Hymel, *All Politics is Local: And Other Rules of the Game* (New York: Random House, 1987). As speaker of the house, O'Neill could have rallied considerable support for Carter's programs, but he never established a working rapport with Carter or his aides, particularly Hamilton Jordan whom O'Neill nicknamed "Hannibal Jerken."
19. Zbigniew Brzezinski memo to Hamilton Jordan [for Carter], 5 July 1977, Hamilton Jordan's Files, Box 35, JCL.
20. "Notes on Meeting with Jewish Leaders," n.a. [possibly Joyce Starr], 6 July 1977, Stuart Eizenstat's Files, Box 235, JCL. A shorter version of these notes is found in Joyce Starr memo (White House liaison on Soviet Jews and Jewish Community Affairs), for the Files, File ND16/CO1–7, Box ND 39, JCL.
21. Louis J.Cantori, "Egyptian Policy," in *The Middle East Since Camp David*, Robert O. Freedman, ed. (Boulder, CO: Westview Press 1984), pp. 171–91. Cantori argues that the inclusion of the Soviet Union in the conference helped motivate Sadat to visit Israel.
22. Landrum Bolling letter to Carter, 20 December 1978, Box ND40, JCL.
23. Carter letter to Abourezk, 2 October 1978, Palestine Liberation Name File; see also Paul Findley, Name File, and WHCF, Box CO-35, JCL.
24. Reports and protests about these meetings are found in Jody Powell's Files, Box 82, JCL.
25. See Alan Hart, *Arafat: Terrorist or Peacemaker?* (London: Sidgwick & Jackson, 1984), pp. 440–1, for a fuller discussion of the background to Young's resignation and the behind-the-scenes negotiations with the PLO.
26. Ed Sanders memo to Hamilton Jordan, 27 August 1979, Staff Offices, Ed Sanders File 8/9/79–10/9/79, Box 1, JCL.
27. Jack Watson (Cabinet Secretary and Assistant for Intergovernmental Affairs), Oral History Project, Miller Center interview, 17–18 April 1981; see also: Zbigniew Brzezinski, Exit interview, 20 February 1981, JCL.
28. Fayez A. Sayegh in *Camp David and Palestine: a Preliminary Analysis* (New York: Americans for Middle East Understanding, 1979), provides a thorough study of the framework's language and content. For a full text of the Framework for Peace see: Carter, *Blood of Abraham*, Appendix 4.
29. Carter, *Keeping Faith*, pp. 300, 325–7, 377.
30. Carter, *Blood of Abraham*, p. 169.

31. Ibid. (For a retrospective view of the Camp David negotiations 25 years later, see: Bob Cullen, "Two Weeks at Camp David," *Smithsonian*, September 2003.)

32. James E. Akins letter to Brzezinski, 24 September 1979, Box CO-8, JCL. Akins was a former U.S. Ambassador to Saudi Arabia.

33. "Into the Valley of the Shadow of Failure," *Events*, 23 March 1979.

34. Ed Sanders and Roger Lewis memo to Robert J. Lipshutz (White House Counsel) and Hamilton Jordan, 11 January 1978, Robert Lipshutz's Files, Box 6, JCL.

35. Ed Sanders to the president and vice president, 6 March 1978, Office Staff, Box 75; Staff Office, Box 1, 3, JCL.

36. Ed Sanders memo to Carter, 15 August 1979, Hamilton Jordan's Files, Box 49, JCL.

37. Hamilton Jordan memo to Carter, 30 November 1978, Hamilton Jordan's Files, Box 49, JCL.

38. Joint Letter to President Carter from President Sadat and Prime Minister Begin, 26 March 1979,.Department of State, Selected Documents, No. 11 (Washington, D.C.: U.S. Government Printing Office, 1979).

39. See *Congressional Record* 124, September 1978; Hyman Bookbinder and James G. Abourezk, *Through Different Eyes Two Leading Americans, A Jew and an Arab, Debate U.S. Policy in the Middle East* (Bethseda: Adler & Adler Publishers, Inc., 1987). Julie Eadeh, "Senator James G. Abourezk and the Failure of the Camp David Accords," December 1998, unpublished paper.

40. Briefing Memorandum, Hodding Carter III (Department of State) to Ambassador Linowitz and Harold Saunders, Assistant Secretary of State, 27 June 1980, WHCF, Box CO-8, JCL.

41. Hodding Carter III to Ambassador Linowitz and Harold Saunders, 27 June 1980, WHCF, CO-8, Middle-Near East, (CO1-7), JCL.

42. Cullen, "Two Weeks at Camp David," p. 64.

11 CURTAIN CALLS: PRESENT AND FUTURE

1. For a well-documented account of Israel's policies and goals in Africa see: Zach Levey, "Israel's Strategy in Africa, 1961–67," *International Journal of Middle East Studies*, Vol. 36, No. I, February 2004. Levey describes Israel's desire for a strategic alliance with the United States and the attempts to use its ties with several key Africa states as leverage and proof of its pro-U.S. stance in the Cold War. Warren Bass in *Kennedy's Middle East and the Making of the U.S.–Israel Alliance* (New York: Oxford University Press, 2003) highlights Israel's failed attempts to convince the Kennedy administration that a military alliance would be in the best interests of both nations.

2. William B. Quandt, *Peace Process: American Diplomacy and the Arab–Israeli Conflict Since 1967* (Washington, D.C.: The Brookings Institution, 1993), p. 380.

Bibliographic Essay

DOCUMENTS

Document collections consulted include: Gerald Ford Presidential Library, Jimmy Carter Presidential Library, Lyndon B. Johnson: National Security Files. Middle East. National Security File, 1963–1969 (Frederick, MD: University Publications of America, 1988), and the Rockefeller Center Archive.

MEDIA

Numerous studies focus on the impact of the media on all branches of the government as well as on the influence of the media in formulating public opinion. The most useful include: James Fallows, *Breaking the News: How the Media Undermine American Democracy* (New York: Pantheon, 1996); Howard Kurtz, *Hot Air: All Talk, All the Time* (New York: Times Books, 1996); and Michael Janeway, *Republic of Denial: Press, Politics, and Public Life* (New Haven: Yale University Press, 1999). Based on extensive historic research, *The Problem of the Media: U.S. Communication Politics in the 21st Century* (New York: Monthly Review Foundation, 2004), by Robert W. McChesney, provides a detailed analysis of the weaknesses of the media. In *Wizards of Media Oz: Behind the Curtain of Mainstream News* (New York: Common Courage 1997), Norman Solomon and Jeff Cohen refute the popular myth that the U.S. media are dominated by liberals. Bernard C. Cohen, in *The Press and Foreign Policy* (Princeton: Princeton University Press, 1963), gives a useful overview of the media and foreign policy coverage. Melani McAllister in *Epic Encounters: Culture: Media, and U.S. interests in the Middle East, 1945–2000*, American Crossroads, No. 6, Berkeley: University of California Press, 2001, analyzes the interrelationship of popular culture and politics with particular attention to the role of religion in the U.S. political landscape. "Peace, Propagands and the Promised Land" (Bathesba Ratzkoff and Sut Jhally, 2004) is a provocative and extremely informative 80 minute video that highlights how Israeli public relations campaigns, in conjunction with domestic interest groups in the U.S., have successfully slanted or distorted news coverage about the Middle East.

Other scholars have described media coverage of the Middle East. Among the best are: Yahya R. Kamalipour, ed., *The U.S. Media and the Middle East* (Westport, CT.: Greenwood Publishing Group, 1995), and Gadi Wolfsfeld, *Media and Political Conflict: News from the Middle East* (Cambridge: Cambridge University Press, 1997). Doreen Kays, *Frogs and Scorpions: Egypt, Sadat and the Media* (New York: HarperCollins, 1985), highlights Sadat's infatuation with media attention.

The works by Jack Shaheen, *Reel Bad Arabs: How Hollywood Vilifies a People* (Northampton, MA: Interlink Publishing Group, Incorporated, 2001), and *The TV Arab* (Bowling Green, Ohio: Bowling Green State University Popular Press, 1984); Reeva S. Simon, *The Middle East in Crime Fiction: Mysteries, Spy*

Novels and Thrillers from 1916 to the 1980 (New York: Lilian Barber Press, 1989) and Janice J. Terry, *Mistaken Identity: Anti-Arab Stereotypes in Popular Literature* (Washington, D.C.: Arab American Council, 1985), give in-depth insights into the anti Arab/Muslim stereotypes common in popular culture.

MAKING FOREIGN POLICY

George Lenczowski, *American Presidents and the Middle East* (Durham, NC: Duke University Press, 1990) is the standard source. John P. Miglietta in *American Alliance Policy in the Middle East 1945–1992* (Lanham, MD: Lexington Books, 2001), focuses on the role of the Cold War and perceived security concerns in influencing U.S. foreign policy decisions in Middle East; he emphasizes the patron–client relationships with Iran, Israel and Saudi Arabia. Avi Shlaim, *A Critique of American Policy* (New York: Whittle Books, 1994), stresses U.S. cooperation with Israel.

PEACE PROCESS

William B. Quandt in *Decade of Decisions: American Policy Toward the Arab–Israeli Conflict, 1967–1976* (Berkeley: University of California Press, 1977) and *Peace Process: American Diplomacy and the Arab–Israeli Conflict since 1967* (Washington, D.C.: The Brookings Institution, 1993) are solid, balanced narratives. *The Quest for Peace: Principal United States Public Statements and Documents Relating to the Arab–Israeli Peace Process, 1967–1983* (Washington, D.C.: Government Printing Office, 1983) is a key primary reference. Mohammed Hassanein Heikal's *Secret Channels: The Inside Story of Arab–Israeli Peace Negotiations* (London: Trafalgar Square, 1997), is a fascinating inside account by a leading Arab journalist. Gil Carl Alroy, *The Kissinger Experience: American Policy in the Middle East* (New York: Horizon Press, 1975); Howard H. Baker, *Peace and Stability in the Middle East: A Report* (Washington, D.C. Government Printing Office, 1975) and Matti Golan, *The Secret Conversations of Henry Kissinger: Step-by-Step Diplomacy in the Middle East* (New York: Quadrangle Books, 1976) deal with the Kissinger years.

ISRAEL AND THE U.S.

W.A. Beling, ed., *The Middle East: Quest for an American Policy* (Albany: New York State University, 1973) and David Schoenbaum, *The United States and the State of Israel* (New York: Oxford University Press, 1993), are solid political overviews. Abraham Ben-Zvi, *Kennedy and the Politics of Arms Sales to Israel* (London: Frank Cass Publishers, 2002), traces the development of the military alliance between Israel and the U.S. Moshe Arens in *Broken Covenant: American Foreign Policy and the Crisis Between the U.S. and Israel* (New York: Simon & Schuster, 1995), focuses on the 1980s from an Israeli perspective; he argues that the U.S. was not supportive enough. On the other side, Gabriel Sheffer in *Dynamics of Dependence: U.S.–Israeli Relations* (Boulder, CO: Westview Press, 1987), stresses the importance of the strategic alliance and Israel's ability to oppose its patron's policies based on its almost unquestioned support in

Congress. Foreign policy adviser to Simon Peres, Nimrod Novik, in *The United States and Israel: Domestic Determinants of a Changing U.S. Commitment* (Boulder, CO.: Westview, 1986), warned of possible negative shifts in U.S. policies toward Israel. Marvin C. Feuerwerger traces Congressional support for Israel in *Congress and Israel: Foreign Decision-making in the House of Representatives, 1969–1976* (Westport, CT: Greenwood Press, 1979).

THE ARABS AND THE U.S.

Paul J. Hare, *Diplomatic Chronicles of the Middle East: A Biography of Ambassador Raymond A. Hare* (Lanham: University Press of America and Middle East Institute, Washington, D.C., 1993) and Richard B. Parker, *The Politics of Miscalculation in the Middle East* (Bloomington: Indiana University Press, 1993), are perceptive accounts of U.S. diplomatic relations with various Arab states by experts in the field. Robert D. Kaplan's *The Arabists: the Romance of an American Elite* (New York: Free Press, 1993), is a hatchet job on the U.S. diplomatic corps and its alleged pro-Arab, anti-Israeli stance.

LOBBIES

The existence of a vast number of publications on lobbies indicates the importance of this subject. Among the foremost general overviews of lobby/pressure groups are: Allan J. Cigler and Burdett A. Loomis, *Interest Group Politics* (2nd edn., Washington, D.C.: CQ Press, 1986). Bernard C. Cohen, *The Influence of Non-governmental Groups on Foreign Policy Making* (Boston: World Peace Foundation, 1959) and *The Public's Impact on Foreign Policy*, (Boston: Little, Brown & Co., 1973); Kenneth G. Crawford, *The Pressure Boys: The Inside Story of Lobbying in America* (New York: Arno Press, 1974); Russell W. Howe and Sarah H. Trott, *The Power Peddlers: How Lobbyists Mold America's Foreign Policy* (Garden City, NY: Doubleday & Co., 1977). Dennis S. Ippolito and Thomas G. Walker, *Political Parties, Interest Groups and Public Policy: Group Influence in American Politics* (Englewood Cliffs, NJ: Prentice-Hall, 1980) as well as H.R. Mahood, *Pressure Groups in American Politics* (New York: Harper & Row, 1967), offer interesting insights. In *Foreign Attachments: The Power of Ethnic Groups in the Making of American Foreign Policy* (Cambridge, MA: Harvard University Press, 2000), Tony Smith contends that these special interest groups have had a largely negative impact on policy.

Ballinger Publishing Company in *The PAC Directories* periodically updates the ever changing and shifting PACs. Bruce I. Oppenheimer in *Oil and the Congressional Process* (Lexington, MA: Lexington Books, 1974), traces the influence of the petroleum industry on the U.S. government.

ZIONIST LOBBIES AND PRESSURE GROUPS

James Deakin, *The Lobbyists* (Washington, D.C.: Public Affairs Press, 1966); Edward Tivnan, *The Lobby: Jewish Political Power and American Foreign Policy* (New York: Touchstone, Simon & Schuster 1987); and Paul Findley, *They Dare to Speak Out: People and Institutions Confront Israel's Lobby* (3rd edn., Westport, CT:

Lawrence Hill, 1985), describe the power and influence of the Zionist lobby; Tivnan and Findley are particularly critical of the Zionist lobby. Likewise, Lee O'Brien in *American Jewish Organizations and Israel* (Washington, D.C.: Institute for Palestine Studies, 1986), presents an overwhelmingly negative analysis of the impact of the Zionist lobby on U.S. policies. The film *The Lobby* by Benny Burner examines the controversial role of AIPAC. In contrast, Abraham Ben-Zvi in *The United States and Israel* (New York: Columbia University Press, 1994) and Yossi Melman and Dan Raviv, *Inside the US–Israel Alliance* (New York: Hyperion, 1994)) highlight the positive aspects of the relationship. In *Jews and American Politics* (New York: Doubleday, 1974), Stephen D. Isaacs and Lee O'Brien describe the political role of Jewish Americans and their relationship with Israel. Peter Golden's *Quiet Diplomat: A Biography of Max M. Fisher* (New York: Cornwall Books, 1992) is a readable account of a particularly influential Jewish American activist.

CYPRUS

Laurence Halley in *Ancient Affections: Ethnic Groups and Foreign Policy* (New York: Praeger Publishers, 1985) focuses on the geo-political factors of the Cyprus conflict. One of the best available studies is Chris P. Ionnides, *Realpolitik in the Eastern Mediterranean: From Kissinger and the Cyprus Crisis to Carter and the Lifting of the Turkish Arms Embargo* (New York: Pella Publishing 2001); Ionnides directly addresses the power politics behind the Cyprus crisis and U.S. responses to it. Chapter 5 of John Spanier and Joseph Nogee, eds., *Congress, the Presidency and American Foreign Policy* (New York: Pergamon Press, 1981), describes the Cyprus crisis; it also contains sections on U.S. policy and Arab Boycott issues. Lawrence Stern's *The Wrong Horse: The Politics of Intervention and the Failure of American Diplomacy* (New York: Times Books, 1977), traces the Cyprus conflict and Turkish arms embargo. Paul Watanabe in *Ethnic Groups, Congress, and American Foreign Policy: The Politics of the Turkish Arms Embargo* (Westport, CT: Greenwood Press, 1984), discusses the role of Greek pressure groups in securing the U.S. arms embargo against Turkey. Dom Bonafede, "Turkish Arms Vote Discourages Staff," *National Journal Reports* 7, 31 (2 August 1975), p. 1118 and Richard C. Campany, *Turkey and the United States: The Arms Embargo Period* (New York: Praeger, 1986) describe the political aspects of the U.S. Turkish relationship.

ARAB BOYCOTT

For the most complete overviews, with extensive documentation on the legal and business aspects and pro-Israeli opposition, see: Sarna, A.J., *Boycott and Blacklist: A History of Arab Economic Warfare Against Israel* (Totowa, NJ.: Rowman & Littlefield, 1986) and Kennan Teslik, *Congress, the Executive Branch, and Special Interests: The American Response to the Arab Boycott of Israel* (Westport, CT: Greenwood Press, 1982). Richard E. Cohen, "The Anti-Arab Boycott Bill – Welcome to Business's Hard Times," *National Journal* 9, 5 (29 January 1977), pp. 160–7; Richard S. Frank, "Arab Boycotts Undermine U.S. Premise," *National Journal Reports* 7, 13 (29 March 1975), p. 477; Paul Lewis,

"Administration is Boycotting Anti-Arab Boycott Bills," *National Journal* 8, 25 (9 June 1976), pp. 855–9, and A.J. Meyer and Thomas R. Stauffer, "The Failings of Anti-Arab Boycott Legislation," *National Journal* 8, 31(31 July1976), p. 1096, offer short descriptions of the economic impacts of the boycott and the campaign against it. William E. Simon, "United States Policy on the Arab Boycott," *National Journal* 8 (31 July 1976), pp. 1092–3, gives the government point of view. "The Arab Boycott Whys and Wherefores," Americans for Middle East Understanding Inc. (n.d., probably c.1977) explains the boycott from an Arab perspective.

THE FORD PRESIDENCY

George Bush and Brent Scowcroft, *A World Transformed* (New York: Alfred A. Knopf, 1998) and Gerald R. Ford, *A Time to Heal* (New York: Harper & Row Publishers, 1979), are key primary sources. John Robert Greene, *The Presidency of Gerald R. Ford* (Lawrence, KS: University Press of Kansas, 1995), is a short overview. E.R.F. Sheehan, "How Kissinger Did It: Step-by-Step in the Middle East," *Foreign Policy*, March 1976, is an extremely readable account of Kissinger's techniques and impact. Mala Tabory, *The Multinational Force and Observers in the Sinai: Organization, Structure, and Function* (Tel Aviv: Jaffee Center for Strategic Studies, Tel Aviv University 1986), is a scholarly study of the complex Sinai agreements.

THE CARTER PRESIDENCY

Zbigniew Brzezinski, *Power and Principle: Memoirs of the National Security Adviser, 1977–1981* (New York: Giroux, 1983); Jimmy Carter, *The Blood of Abraham: Insights into the Middle East* (Boston: Houghton Mifflin, 1984) and *Keeping Faith: Memoirs of a President* (New York: Bantam Books 1982); Hamilton Jordan, *Crisis* (New York: Putnam Publishing Group, 1982); Cyrus Vance, *Hard Choices* (New York: Simon & Schuster, 1983) and Jody Powell, *The Other Side of the Story* (New York: Morrow 1984), are all first-hand accounts of the Carter presidency. Douglas Brinkle, *The Unfinished Presidency: Jimmy Carter's Journey Beyond the White House* (New York: Viking, 1998), is a thoughtful discussion, as is Gaddis Smith's *Morality, Reason and Power: American Diplomacy in the Carter Years* (New York: Hill and Wang, 1986). Burton I. Kaufman, *The Presidency of James Earl Carter, Jr.* (Lawrence, KS: University Press of Kansas, 1993), is part of a presidential series that, in contrast to most others in the series, offers a highly critical assessment of the president. Clark R. Mollenhoff, *The President who Failed: Carter out of Control* (New York: Macmillan Publishing Co., 1980), is similarly hostile. William Quandt's *Camp David: Peacemaking and Politics* (Washington, D.C.: Brookings Institution Press, 1986) and Quandt, ed., *The Middle East: Ten Years After Camp David* (Washington, D.C.: The Brookings Institution Press, 1988), are among the best studies of the Camp David negotiations and agreements.

Index

Compiled by Sue Carlton